Understanding the Human Jesus

Stephanie —
Enjoy The insights
of Cenele's spiritual
direction —
god bless you indeed
god bless you indeed —

Walt Simmons
St. Margaret's
Baltimore —

Andrew Canale

Understanding the Human Jesus

A Journey in Scripture
and Imagination

Paulist Press  *New York/Mahwah*

Library of Congress
Catalog Card Number: 84-61027

ISBN: 0-8091-2654-0

Published by Paulist Press
997 Macarthur Boulevard,
Mahwah, New Jersey 07430

Printed and bound in the
United States of America

Contents

To my wife, Kay McGowan

Introduction
by Morton Kelsey

Who was this Jesus of Nazareth who has made such an impact on history? Who was this man whose life and thought have shaped the ideals, if not the actions, of the Western world? So great was his influence that it transformed a small band of peasants, fishermen and political radicals into a band of men and women who were willing to die for their master. By the power of their love and courage the followers of the Way even conquered the Roman Empire that had persecuted them. Many people throughout the ages, and still today, testify that this human being, the risen Christ of Nazareth, has touched their lives, lifted them out of darkness and given them new and transformed lives.

Throughout the first four centuries of the Christian era the Church wrestled with the question of who Jesus really was. Theology has called the answers to this question "Christology." There were many indications that something more than the ordinary human being was present in Jesus. The great ecumenical councils of the Church affirmed that God out of love for human beings became incarnate in Jesus of Nazareth. He expressed God's essential nature in his life and teaching, in his death and resurrection. Was Jesus human or divine?

The answer to this question made an enormous difference. If Jesus were only God play-acting in order to teach us a lesson, then we human beings could not be certain that God knew the full agony of the human plight. They could well doubt that God truly cared and their hope for salvation might not be fulfilled. On the other hand, if Jesus were only human, could we be assured of his victory over death and evil or of our hope for ultimate and eternal life? The Church found that either/or logic was not adequate to the question.

Jesus was both fully human and fully divine. This great paradox was formulated in the creed of Chalcedon and has been the foundation of orthodox Christianity from the fourth century until the present time.

Most human beings find it difficult to tolerate paradoxes, and so there has been a tendency to emphasize either the human or the divine nature of Jesus. Many of the traditional churches have been confronted during the last three centuries with a secular world skeptical about any divine reality; these churches have often overstressed the divine aspect of Jesus' nature. Relating to pure holiness and unapproachable light is difficult for us earthy human hybrids. The loving God evidently knew our human condition. God became what we are in order that we might become what God is. Paul wrote to the Philippians that although Jesus had the very nature of God, he gave it all up and humbled himself not only to become a human being, but even to death upon a cross. Jesus was of the very nature of God and still completely human.

There is no better way for humans to learn about the essential nature of God than by studying the person of Jesus. We need to know all we can about the humanity of Jesus. We learn about the ultimate nature of reality as we study how Jesus lived, what and how he taught, how he treated women and children, how he stood prophetically against social injustice and religious pettiness, how he healed, how he confronted evil and death, how he died courageously and how he rose again from the dead.

Many revivals in the Church have occurred as Christians have once again immersed themselves in the life and actions of Jesus of Nazareth. The Focolare movement in Italy has pointed to that moment on the cross when Jesus cried out "My God, my God, why have you forsaken me?" as the place where Jesus was most human and most divine. At that time of agony Jesus' humanity touched his divinity most clearly. Many people throughout the ages have discovered the divinity of Jesus as they have meditated on his humanity.

Psychology is the study of our humanness. It is most appropriate that a psychologist, a student of humanness, should speak of the humanity of Jesus. From his knowledge of the depth of human nature, Dr. Canale reveals the incredible depth of Jesus' human nature. In no way does this book deny the divine nature of Jesus, but rather it reveals the divine through the human. The author knows the reality of the present risen Jesus in his own life. He has also found that the risen Christ is the only reality that can help some people as they struggle for light and meaning in depression. In Jesus people can find a fellow sufferer who knew the power of pain, darkness, evil and death and who conquered them in rising again. This one stands at the doorway of our soul ready to enter and share his victory with us.

Dr. Canale knows the depth and breadth of the human person as well as anyone I know. He is one of the most compassionate and skillful therapists I know, one of the few people with whom I can share all of me. In the text he tells how he first realized the unbelievable power and love in the person of Jesus and then through it was led to the ever-present saving power and divinity of Christ. The author has discovered both in his counseling practice and in his lecturing that many people have been turned away and deprived of the meaning and transformation that Jesus can give by the picture of him as unapproachable and only divine. When they are presented with the human side of Jesus they are drawn to this magnificent person whose humanity touches the very core of them. And then they are drawn to his saving power, to his divinity as well.

After the author was touched and renewed by the reality in Jesus of Nazareth, he read all he could about him. He studied biblical criticism and read deeply in Christian theology. However, he does not write as a biblical critic or as a theologian, but as a human being who has felt the impact of Jesus on his own life and on the lives of his clients. He shares the humanity of Jesus that he has discovered, the person who has made such a difference in so many lives. I know of no other book about Jesus like this one. Dr. Canale provides rich insight into the depth of Jesus, and displays the completeness of Jesus' humanity in such a way that we are led to God, the caring divine lover.

Preface

I am passionate about Jesus of Nazareth. In a devastating time during my life, I was shown a way to find his protection. This is painful for me to write and even to admit to myself. It is a sort of coming out of the closet. I don't particularly feel like exposing myself and my feelings in this way and yet I don't know any other way to be truthful. This book is my best attempt to date to be honest. I hope it challenges you and upsets you. I hope that it helps unmask some of your inner turmoil. I hope that it brings you closer to the truth of yourself.

For the truth is good news, excruciatingly good news. There is salvation—if you will give up your life for it. And salvation consists, I think, of finding the courage to live life to the fullest—in the face of its great difficulties. This of course is paradoxical—this giving up of life to have it. And painful too, devastatingly so. I have sometimes railed against God for this, screaming disapproval and anger at all that I and the people that I care for have to suffer. My suffering isn't remarkable—which makes me even angrier in that what I am suffering is simply what people seem to have to suffer. I cry out to God, "Unfair, unfair, blessing and cursing from your mighty throne, allotting hell and heaven at your whim."

But there is Jesus. Jesus confronts this attitude, forces me to examine it, gives hope that the heart of life may be, as he says, a great and generous Lover.

It embarrasses me to admit this. For on the face of it Jesus is woefully wrong. Life usually doesn't seem to stand as evidence for his belief in a merciful loving God. Good people are squashed along with

1

the bad. There is something ultimately evil and malignant that seems to be behind much of life.

Why then am I throwing my support toward Jesus and his perception of the world and God? Simply because I have to if I would be true to my own experience. My senior year at college was the most painful time in my life. It was a time of total uncertainty about career choice and about emotional relationship. I no longer knew what I wanted from life. Life itself seemed stupid and purposeless and no job or relationship seemed capable of changing this. I had been brought up a Roman Catholic in the pre-Vatican II era—when dogma reigned and uncertainty was considered a kind of heresy. The first two years of college I attended Mass faithfully. It wasn't until my junior year one Sunday afternoon when I got up from the table at the library to go to Mass that I seriously questioned the value of attending Mass. A good friend of mine asked me where I was going and I answered him. I will never forget his response, "To Mass! What for?" The question stumped me and I sat back down because I didn't know. For the next two years, I rarely went to Mass and believed it to be an utterly meaningless, superstitious and fraudulent exercise.

This is not to say that I stopped questioning the universe, ceased wondering about what life might mean—because I urgently needed to know. I have never lived well with meaninglessness. I find meaninglessness to be agonizing. It is as if I have a meaning organ within me that agitates when meaning is lost. I cannot stand a universe that is the result of random evolution, where I am the best that life has been able to do so far, where human life ultimately reaches no further than itself and space yawns abysmally toward nothingness.

Yes, I am passionate about Jesus. I am totally subjective. I cannot prove what I believe except by the fact that I am still here—a remarkable fact to me because what I experienced Halloween night, 1970 in my dormitory room at the University of Notre Dame was so destructive and so overwhelming that only transcendent intervention could have saved me. If you find me too dramatic, that is your problem. Recall that I am embarrassed by this myself, and note that embarrassment is usually based on fear of being discovered. And further, consider that belligerence is frequently the other side of fear. So doing, you'll understand where I am emotionally in relation to my personal story and to Christ.

That Halloween night, that night of goblins, vampires and terrors, found me at a movie—during which a sense of unreality came over me. Life seemed tenuous, delicate and with a feeble grasp on me. I felt as though I was going to have a heart attack and die, and I was terrified. I tried to reason with myself, to talk myself out of it—and I momentarily was able to calm myself down. Again the feeling returned near the end of the film, this time with a vengeance. I wanted to scream, to shout out: "I'm dying. Turn off the movie." As soon as the movie ended, I left the auditorium and hurried back to my room, somehow feeling that I would be safer there, but the walls were shimmering, surrealistic. The sizes of different objects were distorted. I paced to and fro, short of breath, panicking, not knowing what to do. I looked out my tenth floor window and saw the reflection of lights in it. I feared being sucked into that world of reflections, being trapped in the window. I knew that I was going mad or dying. Insanity battled heart attack for possession of me. Finally I called a friend and asked him to come and stay with me. When he arrived I burst into tears and he held me while I shared my utter panic with him. After some time, I relaxed and my friend left for a while to sit by the lake to sort things out for himself. I decided to quit school, and I left for home the next morning. After a week there and having made arrangements at the counseling center, I returned to school (because, quite frankly, neither I nor my parents knew what else I could do).

The next three weeks were hell. I consulted a psychologist who reassured me (based on one interview and testing results) that mine was a psychological problem, resolvable by psychological means, and that I could rest assured that I had no spiritual problem. I somehow *knew* that there was a spiritual dimension to my problem. If my problem was only psychological, I felt that my psyche was destroyed beyond recovery. I didn't continue with psychotherapy.

During those weeks, I limped through life, sustained mainly by friendship. Several times I awakened in the middle of the night, panic-stricken. At his prior invitation, I called up my friend who would tell me to start walking and we would meet halfway across campus—as it happened, in front of the main church of the campus. We would then go to his room where he and his roommate would sit up with me—for the rest of the night on a couple occasions.

This friend was a pre-med student who happened to be taking a course called "Pain, Suffering and Death." At one of the class meetings after Halloween, he presented my situation to the class, and the professor offered to meet with me if I desired. An appointment was subsequently arranged for the Monday evening before Thanksgiving.

I arrived for the appointment feeling both hope and trepidation. During the previous three weeks I had told my story to several friends and none of them seemed to fully comprehend it—which left me feeling more isolated, strange and terrified. The meeting had a "last chance" feeling for me. The professor let me into his house and I followed him upstairs to his office. I began to tell him the facts of my story. After a few minutes he stood up, put his hand on my shoulder and said, "I know just what you're talking about. The same thing happened to me twenty years ago." Then he walked over to his desk and returned with a crucifix. "Put this on," he said. "This will protect you against the darkness." Remarkably, I believed him. I took the crucifix and put it on. The combination of finally being understood and of being given the symbol of protection had an immediate effect on me. I felt relieved and hopeful. I drew my first deep breath in three weeks. I knew that I was not alone either humanly or spiritually.

How did I know this? Why did the crucifix give me such reasurance? Was it just my Catholic background? Obviously not, for I had seen several crucifixes during my life and during those three

weeks—with no effect. Was it then due solely to artful psychother-
apeutic maneuvering by the professor? Again, I think not. Something deeper happened. I felt connected to a strong spiritual source
and I don't know why. It does seem to me as if the reality of the crucifix somehow came to me, met me in my desperation, as I sat in the
professor's office.

I do not mean to imply by this story, incidentally, that all my
problems were immediately and magically resolved, nor that mine
was solely a spiritual problem. Ever since, I have struggled with my
life and I have as many psychological problems as the next person.
The point that I am making here is that something happened to me
in that office. Paraphrasing the blind man in John's Gospel, I only
knew that I had been in hell and now I wasn't. And the crucifix—
that grotesque symbol of Christianity—was at the heart of it.

I began to meet regularly with the professor. As we talked about
my experience, I told of my agnosticism and expressed interest in
knowing more about Jesus. He suggested that I read the New Testament from cover to cover. When I did, I was frankly amazed. Jesus
jumped out at me from the pages. I saw a strong, intelligent, compassionate, brilliant, generous, courageous and shamelessly religious
person with the courage to live his belief.

Thus began a thirteen year (thus far) journey toward self-understanding and into Jesus. I have subsequently become a psychologist
whose practice is primarily with people living in turmoil (at least
partly) because of spiritual and meaning problems in their lives. Several of these people have been helped in their struggles when I have
shared with them my vision of the person Jesus. Likewise at several
conferences and workshops where I have presented the following material, people have demonstrated a real hunger to see Jesus' humanity.

And so Jesus has become central in both my professional and
personal life. What is the embarrassment of this for me? Why do I
still have the problem—here I am at a loss for words—claiming him
as Savior? There are several reasons. First of all, I am frankly embar-

rassed by simplistic religion, by literal, Bible-thumping closed-mindedness which labels all other views as heretical and demonic. Remember, I was brought up as a Roman Catholic (and am now a practicing Catholic) in the pre-Vatican II era which proclaimed itself as the sole holder of the truth. This pompous attitude annoys and offends me—and has been destructive to innumerable people. Second, as a psychologist, I have been trained to understand people "scientifically." Speaking out for the power of Christ touches my insecurity as a member of the field. It makes me feel peculiar and different from my peers. I suspect that my fear exposes a certain amount of cowardice on my part to stand up for the truth as I see it. But part of the truth is my fear. Third, to be visibly Christian, to say why I am a Christian, is, as you now understand, a very personal thing. To speak of how Jesus is Christ for me requires that I again confront a time of great brokenness in my life, and this is very painful—as is the sharing of this brokenness with you. For I don't know how you will treat my story. But even that finally doesn't matter.

When I first decided to write this book I didn't realize that I would have to be so self-disclosive. I was, after all, writing a life of Jesus, a life which stood on its own with no need of my story to give it value. Perhaps I envisioned it as a piece of biblical criticism. Frankly, the first versions missed the mark. Next, I tried to speak as a psychologist who is interested in sharing a method of encountering the person Jesus, but still something crucial was missing. Finally, with the helpful criticism of Scott Peck and Morton Kelsey, I realized that what was missing was my passion for Jesus, my amazement, my admiration and my love for the man. I've already told you my hesitations for sharing my passion, but I now see that passion is the way of truth.

What we will encounter in this book is the loving power of the life of Jesus. I do not profess to understand the paradoxical mystery of divinity and humanity. The question has been "resolved" theologically for many centuries that Jesus was truly God and truly man. Roman Catholics as a group have typically honored and "understood" the divinity of Jesus, whereas Protestants have typically "understood" his humanity. Each group has unfortunately rarely listened to the other's expertise. For myself, what is important is the meeting with divinity at the center of one's life. For me, Jesus was the human vehicle and expression of my encounter with God. He has helped me; he has saved me; I was dead and am now alive. The theological questions are moot.

Several people have been instrumental in different ways in the development of this book. Morton Kelsey has read the many versions of the manuscript and has made several helpful critical comments about it. Paul Jamison, who for years was a medical missionary in the Middle East, has provided a virtual gold mine of materials and insights about Jesus and the Holy Land. Tim Kochems has read and discussed the book with me and made several helpful suggestions. I have also discussed the ideas of the book with Doug Daher on many occasions. Sister Frances Scribner and I have dialogued about most of the central ideas contained herein. Lynn Runnells has patiently and effectively typed the manuscript in its many different forms. John Whalen has spent many hours helping me clarify, edit and rework the manuscript. Without his help, I would have had great difficulty resolving the many questions of style, content and form. Scott Peck and Madeleine L'Engle have both made very helpful comments about the manuscript. Finally, my wife Kay has provided support, encouragement, editing, proofreading and time without which I could not have written the book.

Prologue

Every day people tell me stories of meaninglessness, suffering, and desperation. Their relationships aren't working, no one understands them, work isn't satisfying or available, illness has removed their joy in living. Often they have sought psychotherapy as a last resort. They don't know where else to turn or if in fact there is any way out of their present dilemma. Sometimes as I listen, I have to agree with them: on the face of it I can see no solution either. Take, for instance, a woman in her middle thirties with five teenage children whose husband has been disabled for a year and can no longer collect disability. One of her sons has been arrested for shoplifting and her youngest daughter has run away from home. The family needs $300 a week just to meet their bills; she brings home $160. Or consider a man in his forties who hates his present work and feels called by God to the ministry. Though he has received verbal support from church and school officials and from his family, he has not been admitted to seminary and feels he may have to wait forever stuck in his unsatisfactory job. As a third typical example, consider a young woman in the midst of an existential crisis. Raised in a traditional Catholic household, she had through her life abided by the rules and found life to be meaningful and enjoyable. Recently, however, for some unexplainable reason, life has lost all its meaning and dark terrors have assailed her. It is as if evil stalks her and she feels that she will soon go crazy. Suicide has become a viable option except for her Catholic fear of eternal damnation. As she said to me, "I can't get myself out of hell because I will end up in hell for doing so." It was this double bind which brought her into therapy.

The problems expressed in these brief accounts of three lives are not unusual. They are in fact frighteningly commonplace. Ministers, psychiatrists, and psychologists are daily confronted with such problems. The statistics of human suffering are terribly distressing. As one example, the World Health Organization estimates that at any given time approximately three percent of the world's population is clinically depressed. One syndrome alone affects at least one hundred million people in the world. It is no wonder that thinking persons become distressed (and even depressed themselves!) when they consider the world they inhabit. Illness, pollution, economic distress, wars in different parts of the world, and the constant threat of nuclear war all contribute to feelings of hopelessness, dread, and the horrible thought that life itself may be a meaningless quirk in a vast and empty universe.

People must confront these realities and find some explanation which satisfies them. Often this seems so overwhelming as to be impossible. How can one person's thoughts matter in this vast universe? What matters an individual's solutions to these problems? There is a need and a kernel of desperate hope which sends people flocking to psychotherapists and clergy to receive solace and to find answers to these monumental concerns.

Traditional psychotherapy which seeks to explore deep psychological conflict, to promote more adaptive behaviors, and to help restructure thinking patterns often helps persons live more satisfying and productive lives. But in itself, traditional psychotherapy does not confront metaphysical or spiritual questions. At best, traditional psychotherapy acknowledges the value of such questions and takes an agnostic position. At worst, it defines such concerns as moot and maladaptive and strives to make people more "realistic" so that "daily problems" may achieve preeminence in their lives.

The great religious leaders have attempted to confront these crucial questions of the meaning of existence. Jesus and the Buddha, for example, devoted their lives to their particular pictures of what is ultimate in life. Through the centuries, churches and sects have arisen which follow one or another of these great leaders. Members of these churches and sects have sought to discover and to appropriate for themselves what their leaders learned before them. Unfortunately, people are often only marginally successful in this task. The great questions sometimes become clear while the answers remain hidden.

The traditional Church has failed many people who have asked these ultimate personal questions. Afraid of having its authority undermined, the Church has sometimes hidden behind dogma and proclaimed mystery a dangerous province where only experts dare to tread. Regrettably, dogmatic pronouncements by themselves do not solve the questions on which they take their stand. Persons struggling with existential concerns cannot be satisfied by formulas. Rather they need existential solutions.

Traditional psychotherapy and traditional dogmatics fail these existential seekers for reasons given above. An approach that allows for exploration and for the possibility of finding a meaningful solution is necessary to embark on such an adventure. This type of approach unfortunately is fraught with its own dangers. Without the markers of traditional dogma or the guidance of traditional psychotherapy, one enters a dangerous terrain alone. Buddhism names this place *makyo* where one can get lost forever in a welter of horrifying and/or enticing images.

Some sort of guide is obviously needed if a person is to negotiate the territory. A guide is one who knows the terrain, the lurking dangers, the places of refreshment, and the way to the goal. Therefore only one who has traveled the journey successfully can serve another as guide. The importance of having a guide cannot be overstated. There are those hardy few who somehow manage to achieve their goal alone but these heroic individuals are greatly outnumbered by those who fall along the way.

For the Christian making such a journey, it would be of great interest and significance to discover how Jesus faced these universal questions. Christianity as an incarnational religion professes in prin-

ciple the importance of the personhood of Jesus. It is a Christian belief that Jesus took on humanity so to open us to divinity. For the
Christian struggling with existential questions, no consideration of
Jesus is more important than how he handled his own humanity and
resolved for himself what was his own place in the cosmos.

The goal of this book is to explore the humanity of Jesus in order
to see what this tells us about him and about our own humanity and
to offer a potential answer to the existential question which can be
stated thus: What did Jesus see as our place in the cosmos?

Certain tools are necessary if we are to reach our goal. First, we
will need to consult the sources of information about the person Jesus. The most important sources obviously are the Gospels. One of
the problems with the Gospels for our study is that their primary purpose is to proclaim the good news that Jesus is the awaited Messiah—
not to give an exact biography of the person Jesus. The humanity of
Jesus is noted rather to amplify the authors' goal. Nevertheless, a
careful reading gives many clues into his humanity.

Second, biblical critics, historians, and archaeologists have examined the texts and the known history of the time. Some of these
critics have despaired ever knowing the historical Jesus. The Jesus
who appears in the Gospels is, they say, the Christ of faith, embel-
lished by myth beyond recognition as a particular individual. Other
critics emphasize that certain texts, most notably the parables about
the Kingdom of heaven, have the authentic stamp of a particular personality. These sayings, these critics say, at least permit hints and
guesses about Jesus' personality.

We need not be dismayed by the shortcomings of the text, for
they serve to highlight a problem of Christian belief—i.e., somehow
Jesus was fully human and simultaneously in a unique parent-child
relationship with God. This very problem encourages the Christian
who is in an existential crisis or searching for meaning because it of-
fers the hope of finding a positive and saving relationship with God
through living one's humanity fully rather than by denying it.

The third tool of our study comes from psychology. Psychology is a critical resource for at least two reasons. First of all, twenty centuries separate us from the life of Jesus, and as much as seventeen centuries separate us from dogmatic pronouncements about Jesus' humanity and divinity at the Councils of Nicaea (A.D. 325) and Chalcedon (A.D. 451). It is difficult for many present strugglers to be satisfied by these pronouncements. Rather, being presented with the credal formulation that Jesus was "truly God and truly man," they may answer "So what? This doesn't help me with *my* life problems." These people are stating that they need something that touches their psyches, that they can experience as authentic. It does not matter to them, for instance, that Athanasius had a deep spiritual experience that he put forth in the Creed. Unless their own souls are touched, credal statements serve merely to amplify their pain and their sense of meaninglessness and disconnection.

Related to this need for psychological experience is the fact that psychology has developed methods for reaching normally hidden aspects of the psyche or soul. Two of these methods are relaxation and imagination. Relaxation enables persons through deep breathing and concentration to put aside their present concerns momentarily and to look within themselves for new solutions and for new insights. Imagination furthers this process by bringing forth pictures, images, and stories that expose the workings of a person's soul.

In the present book, we will be using imagination in a number of ways. It will help us enter into the accounts of Jesus' life and be a part of these events. It will allow us to bring together biblical and historical data so that we may picture the setting and the events. It will further allow us to step out onto a ledge and reflect on events that are not explicitly recorded in the Gospels. For instance, we will imagine what Jesus may have experienced in the desert before his public ministry and what his own experiences were that led to his teachings and stories. Obviously, imagination will not recapture the precise historical moment but it may suggest what Jesus' struggles were and how he resolved the deep questions of life.

Imagination has had a checkered history in religious circles.

One approach toward using imagery is expressed by the great mystic St. Teresa of Avila. She writes: "Imagination is the fool in the house." This view considers imagination to be fanciful, misleading, and potentially dangerous. William Blake, the great English mystic and poet, takes the opposite stance when he writes: "Imagination is the eternal." Two more radically different evaluations of imagination can hardly be imagined. Both have merit. Imagination can be used to mislead and for destructive purposes; it can keep people from facing their lives. But imagination can also open persons to the depths of themselves and to the abiding presence of God. Jesus knew this and used imagery in his parables to show people the Kingdom of God. In fact, Jesus *needed* parables and imagery to make the Kingdom known. Using imagination as one of our tools has then the added benefit of giving us an "insider's view" of the process that Jesus used when formulating his parables about the Kingdom that, as we have noted above, are considered by biblical critics to be those statements that are most certainly his own.

For those still concerned about the use of imagination to discover the person Jesus, let them consider that imagination is ubiquitous. Like it or not, imagination is a part of every aspect of our lives. Our prejudices, beliefs, and emotions are all informed by imagination. Behavioral medicine and psychology have discovered, for example, that negative imagery often contributes to a negative outcome of illness. By fostering positive imagery, individuals are better able to come to grips with their illness and sometimes make dramatic improvements and even unexpected recoveries. If we remember that imagery introduces us to a different non-analytical level of reality and do not demand that it provide us with historical or analytical certainty, we will be rewarded and enriched by our study.

We will begin by using imagery to enter into a powerful moment in Jesus' life. We will then consider the setting, historical data and background of first century Palestine where Jesus lived. Then we will examine in turn the teaching, the stories, the healing works, and the prayer life of Jesus. Next we will turn to how he dealt with love, anger, and fear. We will then examine the crucifixion based on what we have discovered about Jesus the person and on historical data. An imaginative encounter with the resurrection will follow and we will then conclude with some thoughts about the life of Jesus and what it can show the modern person who is searching for meaning.

Evidence shows that imagination is best facilitated by an attitude of quiet openness. Let us now as we embark on this imaginative journey first become quiet within ourselves. By sitting in a comfortable position and taking two or three deep breaths, a feeling of relaxation begins to emerge. The inner chatter becomes noticeable and then grows quiet except for random fleeting concerns. Let them pass by, give them little notice, and feel the tension and stress draining out of your body and being replaced by quiet relaxation. Sit still for a short time and enjoy these feelings before turning to Chapter 1.*

*For several different techniques of relaxation consult the following: H. Benson, *The Relaxation Response.* New York: William Morrow and Co., Inc., 1975. J. White and J. Fadiman, *Relax.* New York: Dell Publishing Co. Inc., 1976. D. Bresler with R. Trubo, *Free Yourself from Pain.* New York: Simon and Schuster, 1979.

1.

The Death of Jesus: The Quiet Agony

It is perhaps unusual that a study of the person Jesus begin with his final agony. I think this is as it should be, however, for several reasons. First of all, as Christians we celebrate Jesus' death every time we gather for Eucharist. The image of the man nailed to the cross is burned into our psyches. Second, we proclaim that his death is somehow related to our salvation. Third, it is an utterly human picture: Jesus has been systematically destroyed in a way that only we humans could devise. Fourth, as I explained in the Preface, the crucifix was for me quite literally the beginning—it was the gift of a crucifix that opened up the possibility of salvation and transformation to me.

We will begin together by entering the quiet torture of the cross. Let us first remember the setting. Pilgrims had gathered in Jerusalem for the feast of Passover. After entering the city to great acclaim the previous Sunday, Jesus had been daily very visible at the temple, teaching, preaching and challenging the religious authorities who then decided that Jesus was so dangerous that he must be silenced. On Thursday evening, Jesus celebrated the traditional Passover meal with his disciples and then went with them to the garden of Gethsemane. After considerable spiritual anguish because of his upcoming torture, he was arrested, deserted by Peter and the other disciples, and taken in turn before the Jewish Sanhedrin, Pilate

17

and Herod. It was determined that he was to be crucified along with two Jewish thieves. He was scourged and then forced to drag his cross to the place of execution where over the next several hours of crucifixion he is reported to have uttered seven statements. According to the Gospels, he asked forgiveness for his persecutors, welcomed one of the crucified thieves into the Kingdom, comforted his mother and his most beloved disciple, cried out in anguish, forsakenness, and traumatic thirst, recognized that his task was finished and gave himself into God's hands.

Obviously, an inner process occurred that brought forth from Jesus these seven utterances from the cross. After his ordeal in Gethsemane, a quietness had come over him. He had had little or nothing to say to his accusers and tormenters thereafter. His death was, in many ways, an inner ordeal—a struggle with more than torture, for he had to face both the rejection of his message and the purpose of his lifework. Perhaps the Adversary that he had met in the desert before he began his public ministry came again to torment him. We will now consider what might have been in his mind during these horrible hours of crucifixion.

Picture him then hanging on the cross, roughly affixed to it by nails, his long hair stuck by sweat and blood to his face. Picture his torn and brutalized body unable to squirm, to get more comfortable. Let yourself enter into his psyche to be with him in his torment. Ponder the tortured thoughts which may have come to him.

. . . Where are you, Abba? My body screams with pain. They have beaten me nearly to death and now this finishes me. They have rejected the Kingdom. I have failed! It is almost too much to bear. I have shown them the power and the beauty of the Kingdom but they would not see it. They did not see you. I have failed to bring you before them. Oh Abba! I am sorry they cannot see you. Abba, let them be, forgive them. They *cannot* know what they are doing. . . .

My body aches, cramps. How can I feel this much pain? They shout and laugh at me. They curse me. Abba! They say that I'm a deluded fool, that I have lied. I am dying. The pain of my two dying brothers here curses you. They are cursing you. Oh, they do not know, they cannot, for it would be impossible for them to say such things about you. That one, what! Listen, he talks to me. Pull me out of this to tell him. With me, with us, in the Kingdom . . .

(A long empty silence.) The taunts are fewer, worthless; there is no point. They have already killed me. Their taunts open me to the silence, to the real battle. The gates of hell vibrate with power, are bursting. Dispossessed demons are laughing. Satan, the Adversary, stands before me.

A: *It is all lost, my friend. I promised you a kingdom once. Look at you now.*

My arms are cramping, the weight of my body pulls me down, tears my hands.

A: *You should have listened to me, my friend. Only the kingdom which is a* kingdom *can come. I have won without you. This world is mine, no matter what your Abba would do. Why it is in your own stories, fool. Even the son was killed by the vineyard workers. You saw it. You could have been king but you washed Peter's feet and he, true to form, deserted you.*

Peter! He stepped out onto the lake. Peter! So afraid that he had to lie, to deny me.

A: *So frightened that love was not enough. Forget it! Love does not work.*

. . . My mother and John stand at my feet. Courage and pain have brought them here. Oh! her heart is breaking. She is left all alone even as I left her in Nazareth. She will be like that poor widow in my story. Have faith, both of you! I cannot reach down to you. John's heart is breaking. I would pull him again to my breast . . . but now I cannot. I cannot comfort him. Unless I give them to each other . . . (The silence continues. Seconds pass slowly. Pain encircles. Cool air comes with the descending darkness.)

> A: *Ah, darkness, my friend. At least I am here with you in hell. Abba is gone, defeated. I gave you three chances but you refused and refused and refused. Those nails must hurt! They tear your skin, your muscles. What a beating you have taken! This is the reward of love.* This *is the Kingdom! Hosanna, hosanna! They threw the palms before you! King! It is written above your head! What can this gathering darkness mean but no to you! Jest of the people, you are more worm than man!*

All who see me jeer at me and sneer.

> A. *Listen to them! You relied on Yahweh. Fool! Let Yahweh rescue you!*

Oh Holy One, in you our fathers put their trust!

> A. *Enslaved people! Roman servants! I offered you the way, the power.*

Yahweh! Abba! I have no one to help me!
. . . No answer comes from Abba. The Adversary retreats. The darkness darkens within me. I feel lightheaded. My blood is leaving me. Darkness fills my heart. The Adversary has crawled inside me. The thorns dig into my head. The thorns in my head!

I am dying. There is only darkness. Pain. My head screams. The salt of my blood is on my lips! The thorns! It is dark. My head screams. The thorns! The Kingdom crashes down around me. Oh darkness. Dare I scream out? What prayer can help me? They jeer, Yahweh! Abba! Abba!

There is only darkness, dried blood, torn flesh. The thorns are tearing my head open! I cannot breathe!

A. *Alone you are, my friend. You are spittle, excrement, waste.*
You have lied to all of them and now they see. Curse them!
Curse them! Free yourself from Yahweh who has gone.
Scream—give in to my silence.

The nails have trapped me. The Adversary grows before me
until my vision blurs. Something deeper than crucifixion tortures me. The Adversary is a gaping tear. The thorns, the nails,
my back, my God! . . .
. . . I hear thunder. Are words hidden there? Or have I lost
Abba? I am so thirsty. My blood drains out of me, my hands,
my head.
How long can this last? I cannot swallow. My skin burns.
My throat, my bowels, I am on fire!

A: *It is only what is promised, friend. You said it yourself. Now*
Abraham's bosom will not hold you.

I cannot swallow. I need to swallow. My body is on fire. I
can feel each wound, each tear, each bruise, and they are all
shouting. Death cannot be far away. I cannot swallow. I have no
spit, Yahweh. I am drained. I am dying. I cannot swallow! Oh
I must drink . . .
. . . What is happening to the pain? Where is my Adversary? Where is my thirst? John holds my mother. The other two
are groaning. Look at all of them watching me. They are so silent. The taunts have dissolved. They are watching me die.
I am dying.
The pain has burst. John holds my mother. I am dying. It
is what I came to do and it is done. Everyone is silent. Even the
Adversary is silent. Some beat their breasts. Oh I would comfort
them if I could!
. . . Alone now. The end comes. I can no longer see them.
A great silence fills and surrounds me. Not even the Adversary
comes to this place of nothingness. This place beyond death and
hatred and hopelessness. This uncreated place.

The pain is only at the edges now. The kind darkness
blinds me as deadness spreads through me. The quiet vacancy is
. . .
Filled! Abba! You are here too! Your arms open, beseech-
ing, welcoming me! You have come to die with me, to be with
me in the deepest darkness. You are here, even here . . .

2.

The Person

What prepared Jesus for his death? What enabled him to suffer through the indignities and tortures as he did? How did Jesus' way of living affect the way he died? We will examine different aspects of Jesus' public life in the following chapters to answer these questions. But the available material about Jesus in the Gospels raises other questions. What happened in Jesus' life before he began his public ministry? What events in childhood and adolescence affected him? Did he have special relationships with certain people? Was his life different from that of other Jewish boys? Did he have a special conscious relationship with God from the beginning?

Almost no data exist to inform us on these questions. Jesus did not suddenly appear full grown at the River Jordan. He had a background; we just don't know many of the specific details. We do know however something about the historical background and setting of first century Palestine and about the typical life style of Palestinian peasants. Since Jesus grew up in this society, he would have been deeply influenced by it. Thus, the life style of typical first century Palestinian Jews indirectly gives us information about Jesus.

At the same time we are arguing that Jesus lived a radically different life. Typical background information by itself gives an insufficient picture of Jesus. I believe that Jesus grew up in a traditional Jewish village, that he was exposed to traditional Jewish thoughts and customs and that something powerful moved him which caused him to dramatically change his life. It was this powerful experience perhaps that sent Jesus south toward Jerusalem and toward John the Baptist. Two themes work together in the present chapter. First, background data of first century Palestine provides a general context for understanding the person who emerged in his public ministry. Second, the clash between his public message and this traditional background suggests the struggle which must have confronted him when he felt called to proclaim his new message. We will consider imaginatively in the last part of the chapter how these two themes worked together to help Jesus ready himself for his public life.

THE JEW

Perhaps the most certain piece of biographical information about Jesus is that he was Jewish. This one fact already tells us much about his background, his thinking patterns, and the issues with which he was concerned. We will now look specifically at several factors which were important in the Jewish culture during Jesus' lifetime.

Chosenness

As a Jew, Jesus was above all one of the "chosen people" of God who expected God to send the Anointed One, the Messiah, to save them. Being chosen can simultaneously be a blessing and a curse. As the "chosen people" the Jews experienced themselves as in special relationship with God who would work through them to effect the salvation of the world. To be thus chosen would give people a sense of deep purpose and belonging. But chosenness usually has its cost. Chosen people are often resented and hated by those who feel excluded and unchosen.

The story of Joseph and his brothers in Genesis (37:2–35) shows both sides of the experience of chosenness. When Joseph told of his dreams in which the sun and moon and eleven stars bowed down before him, and of his brothers' sheaves bowing down to his sheaf, his brothers were furious with him. Because his father Jacob loved him specially and gave him a beautiful coat of many colors, his brothers in their jealousy seized the chance to do away with him. It was the very fact of chosenness that put Joseph in danger.

Captivity

As a chosen people, the Israelites through history have, like Joseph, been resented, hated, enslaved, and thrown into captivity. In Jesus' time, the Romans exercised power over the Jews and military control over Palestine. Roman rules and law thus interfered with the free experience of being God's beloved people. By special agreement the Jews were not conscripted into the army, but taxes were collected for Rome and the Jews had to endure such indignities and sacrilege as when money was taken directly from the temple funds to build a viaduct in Jerusalem. Not surpisingly, Israelites came to power who agreed to do Rome's bidding, while others rose up in protest against foreign domination and sought the overthrow of Rome. When Pilate massacred a group of Jews when he first entered Jerusalem, the anger and horror of the people gave more support to the Zealots who wanted to overthrow Rome.

Messianic Expectations

During this time of domination, the messianic expectations of the chosen people focused on the figure of a conqueror, one who like the Maccabees two centuries before would overwhelm the oppressive regime and crush it, re-establishing Israel as a self-ruling kingdom. Mark tells us that early in his ministry, Jesus again and again warned those he healed not to tell anyone. Did he do this to avoid being seen as the conquering Messiah? Certainly messianic expectations were at a fever pitch. After the feeding of the five thousand (Jn 6:15), men tried to take him forcefully so that he might lead them. In those days (as now) the word Messiah was loaded with meaning. So much was this the case that to use that particular term brought forth such powerful expectations and images that a new meaning could not be given to it. Perhaps Jesus, sensing his own particular call, saw the danger of adopting a title so defined by the expectations of his people. If he indeed saw himself as having a special mission that differed from these messianic expectations, he could not announce it by openly proclaiming himself Messiah but rather by *living* his call and by showing in his actions and his teaching what he had discovered about God and life. To use the word Messiah elicited a set of Jewish expectations and longings which he apparently had no interest in fulfilling.

The Law and Ritual Cleanliness

As a Jew, Jesus was a follower of the law. The rules and expectations of the law were part of the fabric of daily life in Jewish society. Partly because of pagan domination in Jesus' time, ritual cleanliness had become especially important in certain sectors of the population. The community of Pharisees believed that strict adherence to these rules was obligatory for all who would be saved. Out of this attitude grew a rigid literalism—people were judged strictly by their outer behavior. Those people who in small or large ways, for good reasons or bad, failed to keep the letter of the law were considered outsiders whose uncleanliness could be ended only through prescribed ritual actions.

Several professions made persons unclean by their practice. Herdsmen, for example, were looked down upon because it was virtually impossible for them to keep all the rules of ritual cleanliness in their work. Women who were prostitutes were also continuously unclean and therefore scorned. By far the most scorned and devalued profession was that of the publican and tax collector—for not only did these people mingle with the Gentiles, they also made a profit at the cost of their people. The position of the publican was sold to the highest bidder. The publican's profit margin was the difference between what he collected and what he had bid for the position. The publican was thus both a symbol of pagan domination of the Jews and a traitor who turned this domination to his personal advantage. No wonder the Jews treated as outcasts these publicans and tax collectors.

Racial Purity

Racial purity was also extremely important to the Jews of Jesus' time, and thus knowledge of one's genealogy was crucial. Rules about purity enabled the conquered Jews to keep their integrity as God's people while living among the Gentiles. Ability to marry priests and members of legitimate families was based solely on purity of lineage. "Issah" families were those whose legitimacy—the purity of their lineage—was in doubt. People with grave racial blemish (the *pesule qahal*) were called "the excrement of the community." The Samaritans were the most hated of enemies, because they were Jews who had married outside of the faith during captivity and worshiped not at Jerusalem but on Mount Gerizim.

Only those people then without racial blemish or ritual uncleanliness had rights in the Jewish community. Jesus' own legitimacy was never called into question during his ministry. It appears that he was accepted as a son of the house of David and as a legitimate Jew. This is important because had he not been considered a full Jew, no legitimate Jew would have listened to him. What troubled people was his flagrant violation of social mores and custom, his mingling with tax collectors and sinners, his seeming disdain for those rules of purity and cleanliness that excluded some members of the population.

Jesus was thus born into a closed society with rigid rules, where birthright was primary and hatred of others was excused and even expected on the basis of these rules. This social rigidity is understandable when we remember that the Jews were struggling to retain their identity as a people. There is a natural tendency to exclusiveness in each human being which is an expression of that need for order and certainty, for a measuring stick by which to judge good and bad. When someone breaks a social norm by which people order their lives, people are angered and even threatened because they depend on those norms for security. When Jesus sat at table, that most sacred of shared experiences in the Middle East, with sinners and tax collectors, he violated one of his society's sacred norms. Even if Jesus was right in so doing he was challenging the very order of his society. No wonder many Jews were furious with his behavior.

IN NAZARETH

Jesus' home after his return from Egypt as a small boy was the little town of Nazareth. Up to the time of his public life reported in the New Testament, Jesus apparently spent his day to day life there. Aside from the yearly journey to Jerusalem for Passover and perhaps for the Feast of Tabernacles and for Pentecost, his knowledge of the world came from his local surroundings.

As we will discuss more fully in a later chapter, Jesus was a master storyteller. Storytelling was a way of passing on tradition and it was also a break and entertainment in the otherwise somewhat drab existence of village life. Jesus' parables show a keen eye for detail, which he probably developed in early life. Thus village feasts, seeds, yeast and vineyards were some of the images he used to communicate his message of the coming of the Kingdom. Such aspects of everyday life in Nazareth apparently taught him about nature and God and he passed his insights on in his stories.

Perhaps early in his life in Nazareth Jesus was struck by the inconsistency between a society that excluded certain types of people and a God who sent rain on the good and bad alike. Perhaps he was like any other precocious child and constantly needed to know "why." Little Jesus might have asked his parents questions like,

"Why can't I bring this tax collector for dinner, daddy? Why do the men and women sit separately in the synagogue? Why does yeast make bread rise, mommy? Is the whole bush already in that little seed? Why does everyone hate the Romans?" Such questions are natural for little children, springing forth from their curiosity. It would have been hard for his parents to answer most of these questions without being confronted with the social norms and taking a stand for or against these norms. An imaginary dialogue between Jesus and his father on the first question might have continued as follows:

Joseph:	Well, Jesus, my son, people don't like tax collectors because they take our money to Rome.
Jesus:	Why do they take our money?
Joseph:	They say it is to build roads and to protect us.
Jesus:	Why do they not hate you for taking their money when you do carpentry work for them?
Joseph (*pause*):	Because people don't feel that I am forcing them to do something they don't want. They say the tax collector steals from them because he is their enemy.
Jesus:	Then why do they not make him their friend so that he will not want to do this to them?
Joseph (*frustrated*):	Oh Jesus! Go and invite the man to dinner.

Of course this dialogue is drawn from my imagination and not from any written record. But it does not seem antithetical to the character of the adult Jesus. In this fantasy Jesus forces his father to make a decision: he must either stand firm in the social norm and refuse to invite the tax collector to dinner, or incur the wrath of the townspeople for allowing the tax collector to sit at table with his family. Surely the whole town would be quickly informed of this invitation and would surround their little house demanding that Joseph explain this unacceptable behavior. Every action was closely watched and any aberrant behavior was soon known by the whole community. The village life of Nazareth obviously had a powerful effect on Jesus' development. Images from daily village life are present in all his teachings and stories. In his public life, Jesus was drawn to ordinary people. Indeed, his own apostles were typical villagers. Probably most of Jesus' relationships with the people of Nazareth were positive. He deeply understood the longings and desires of people wherever he traveled during his ministry; this affinity and compassion for others must have developed during his long years in Nazareth.

We know that Jesus' father was a carpenter and that Jesus followed him in this profession. It was common in Palestinian society for a son to learn and eventually take over his father's business. There were simply not many career options. A boy did not become a landowner, for instance, if he was not from a family which already owned land. Only members of certain families could become priests or Levites. Children of poor families and those with moderate income very early were expected to help with the family trade. On the positive side, children became familiar at a young age with their life work and so more quickly developed the needed skills.

Jesus must have spent much of his time with Joseph in his shop, learning to use carpentry tools. He must have traveled with his father from an early age to meet his customers. All the people in the town would have identified him as the carpenter's son, one day himself to be a master carpenter. No wonder the people of Nazareth had difficulty in believing in Jesus when he returned home (see, e.g., Mark 6:1–6). In their minds, he had been a carpenter ever since he was a youngster. How could he possibly use his hands for healing?

It is likely that Jesus early identified himself with the carpentry trade, that his imagination pictured him as an adult carpenter rather than a man in some other profession. During most of his adult life, until he began his public ministry, he continued to ply his trade in

Nazareth. There is no biblical evidence that he was unhappy, incompetent or unreliable in his work. Quite likely, he spent his teens and twenties living a practical and typical village life, helping to support his family and carrying out his responsibilities.

THE GALILEAN

Nazareth was located in Galilee north of Jerusalem and was separated from it by Samaria. Galilee was well known in those days as a hotbed of political passion. Leaders of revolts against Rome, would-be Messiahs and Zealots frequently came from there. Quite naturally, the powerful men in Jerusalem worried about these upstarts who threatened the social order and might bring down the wrath of Rome upon Israel. There was a certain suspicion in Jerusalem of all things Galilean.

Galileans were not only potentially dangerous; they were also "provincial." Jerusalem, the sacred city and the home of Yahweh, was the site of all that was important in Jewish life. The question about Jesus "Can anything good come from Nazareth?" (Jn 1:46) was perhaps rhetorical; the expected answer was, "No, nothing good can come from there, so let us not take the man seriously." Galileans were the "rednecks" of the Jewish world; they were good folk and loyal Jews but beyond that they had nothing (so it was thought) to recommend them. Thus Galileans were in the curious position of feeling that they were chosen but not particularly so. They were both insiders and outsiders.

Under these conditions Jesus grew to manhood. The Scriptures taught that his people were the chosen people of God, but there was this nagging feeling among Galileans that others were considered *more* chosen. He may have turned this over in his mind as he thought about the nature of God and about the stirrings in his own heart.

That something must have stirred cannot be denied. Cultural expectations and custom dictated that he would be a carpenter. His family situation required that his earnings be used to help support their day to day needs. Leaving his family placed an extra burden on them. Further, he must have experienced the disapproval and quite possibly the rejection of the townspeople for deserting his family. Something powerful indeed must have shaken him that he would leave the security of home to begin a public ministry under these circumstances.

THE CALL

Thus far in this chapter we have been considering several historical and social factors that must have contributed to Jesus' development. None of these factors in themselves explain why Jesus left home and chose his particular path. Certainly numerous persons before him had been singled out by God for specific reasons. Abraham, Sarah, Moses, Ruth and Jeremiah are five of many such persons mentioned in the Old Testament. Typically, people who were called to proclaim God's message were "disturbed" or "unsettled" in their everyday lives. God called Abraham to leave his home and go to a new land. Moses had the awesome experience of the burning bush where he confronted the holiness of God and was given his mission to lead the Israelites from Egypt.

Jesus probably had one or several powerful experiences himself which unsettled him, left him unsatisfied with his daily life and sent him on his search for God.

This call from God must have stirred him deeply, bringing to the surface several conflicting feelings. Throughout Jewish history, God had surprised the Jews by calling humble persons to accomplish great things. But was it possible that a carpenter from Nazareth was specially chosen? God often made difficult requests of those chosen to do these great works. And yet, how could Jesus be sure that it was God that called him forth? Jesus understood the workings of Nazareth; his support system and family were there. At the same time, his life no longer satisfied him. Perhaps his concentration was disturbed so that he sometimes neglected his work. Perhaps he awakened in the middle of the night—aware of the stirring. Perhaps he was drawn to solitude away from the village where he could open himself to the call. Loyalty to family must have wrestled with the growing power of the call until he must have realized that he would not rest until he answered his inner stirring, that it was futile to try to forget it, that he must follow it because in it lay his meaning in life. And so, with deep uncertainty of where he was being led, Jesus set out from Nazareth heading south toward Jerusalem and the great desert where he would meet John the Baptizer preaching by the River Jordan.

Baptism

The Synoptic Gospels begin their account of Jesus' adult life with his baptism in the River Jordan by John. As we have been considering in our imaginative picturing of his early years, Jesus did not just spontaneously appear at the river—his history and his experience led him there. The Baptist preached the need for repentance and to this Jesus submitted. During his long journey to Judea, he had had time to ponder what was happening to him. Now he saw John and heard his words. Certainly this man in camel-skin clothing had a special message; the crowds around him were immense, and even Pharisees and scribes were there.

Jesus heard the call to repentance and went forth for baptism. Why did he do that? Had he anything to repent? The English word repent derives from Latin *poena,* meaning pain. To repent would be to feel the pain of one's action again. In this sense, Jesus may have repented at his baptism for he had hurt others by following God's call and had felt this pain again himself. Did he then step into baptism out of his need to be affirmed by God? Did he need to be "forgiven" for doing what he was called to do? It was not a wrong action for which he repented but a painful one which he brought to God for healing.

According to Mark's version (1:9–11), Jesus stepped out of the water after he was baptized and "saw the heavens torn apart and the

Spirit, like a dove, descending on him, and a voice came from heaven saying, 'You are my son, the Beloved; my favor rests on you.' " This is a violent passage. The heavens were torn apart; something powerful and out of the ordinary happened. Might we understand the words that Jesus heard as a direct answer to his concerns? He had left home and family. Perhaps after his long journey he felt repentant and unhappy. Now the One who had called him came and claimed him, saying in effect: "You feel you are without family or friends, called alone into the unknown. Even though you are sad, pained and frightened you have come. You are my dear Beloved Son."

The stirring that had brought him from Nazareth began to take a more definite shape. God had affirmed him in his decision to leave home. He now needed to understand the implications of his experience.

The Desert

The Spirit drove him into the wilderness to be by himself (Mk 1:12) and there he remained for forty days. Thus his journey through the desert paralleled the Israelites' forty-year journey to the promised land. The number forty here signifies at least two things: a time of holiness and search, and a very long time. Forty days in lonely spiritual search *is* a long time. But Jesus had much to assimilate. His old life was apparently over; he had left it behind and had been given a new message of sonship from God. What did this mean? How was he to proceed? Should he follow the Baptist's lead and retire to the desert? That somehow didn't seem true to his nature. He didn't want to leave normal daily life but rather to bring God's message *into* it. Surely that would be difficult; he had seen before he left Nazareth that it is a difficult thing to bring the unexpected into everyday life.

So he sat on the rocks under the hot sun and walked the barren desert listening to the silence. Slowly, painfully, his Nazareth life melted away; he shed that old skin like a snake of the desert. Then came that infinite time between what was lost and what is to be found. Patiently, fearfully, he listened and saw new images, new possibilities move before his eyes. He watched them changing, slipping, taking form, following dead ends until the message of belovedness, that he had heard as John baptized him, grabbed hold of him—first subtly and then with great and growing power. "God loves me! I am a humble carpenter from Nazareth and yet God loves me. Even as I starve in the midst of the heat and danger I can feel it—God loves me! I've left my family to fend for themselves—with God—and God loves me! I'm beloved, a son of the Center of the Universe! The Creator is like a daddy to me, a loving parent who accepts me though my family feels I've squandered all that is valuable. I'm welcomed home! Everyone is welcomed home. THAT IS IT! I must tell them that we are dear children of the Most High, that we are *already* forgiven, that the repentance that the Baptist calls for is guaranteed!"

Thus a dramatic culmination of his journey from Nazareth occurred. The agitation that he had felt in Nazareth, the stirring which had demanded something from him, had been answered dramatically. The Spirit had pushed him toward the desert for presumably the same reason that he had had to leave Nazareth. A great new message was being born in him which could not be heard clearly while he remained enmeshed in his everyday life. Something new had entered him which he now saw also wanted to enter everyday life. Just as he experienced himself as precious to God, so did he sense the preciousness of everyone else to God. It was crucial that he bring this message to them that would change their lives; this new understanding of God brought new life. If Jesus could make himself be heard, if people could realize that they were beloved, a new Kingdom would come to be, a Kingdom of God where no one was enslaved or captive and where each person felt beloved.

The Adversary

Jesus left the desert with this great insight. But what was he to do with it? How was he to live it out? As he pondered this question, there before him on the edge of the desert, between him and his new life, stood his Adversary. Suddenly Jesus realized that this figure which stood before him did not want to let him pass. The Adversary, in the distance, looked like a man about his age and size; in fact, from a distance it seemed as though he was approaching himself. As he drew nearer the Adversary, Jesus could sense the great power that came from him. The Adversary looked as though he knew everything about Jesus, understood what had occurred at Jesus' baptism and in the desert. His very person stood as a challenge before Jesus that he could not avoid.

There was a long silence during which each opponent sized up the other. Then the Adversary spoke slowly and deliberately. "Well, my hungry friend, put your power to good use and turn this stone to bread."

Could he? Jesus wondered. His mouth watered at the thought of food but—slowly . . . all else had been done carefully—he weighed the question against his new-found insights and saw that he must not take advantage of what was given him, for Scripture said "Man does not live by bread alone." Did not his need to leave Nazareth already prove that?

"True enough, my friend, and well answered," responded the Adversary. "However, this is your chance. Could you not now rule the world and bring this message to all with power? Give me your allegiance and this I will do for you."

Again he meditated. He did feel powerful. He had made a crucial discovery. But he could not force anyone to understand. God had stirred in him, come to him in his very depths. The Romans and the leaders of his own people tried to force their rules on the people. They, it seemed to him, had taken the Adversary's suggestion and it hadn't brought God to them or to the people. Again he answered from Scripture: "No, you must worship God alone."

Finally the Adversary seemed to grow before him, challenging him: "Are you indeed favored by God and do you indeed believe

Scripture? Then throw yourself from this hill, for Scripture says: 'He will put his angels in charge of you to guard you.' "

But was this the purpose of the gift, Jesus thought, to be glorified himself and to use the forces of God for his own ends? "No," he answered the final challenge. "It has been written: 'You must not put the Lord your God to the test.' "

The Adversary then stepped aside and allowed Jesus to pass. No more questions were asked. Jesus left the desert prepared to tell people the news of their belovedness in the new Kingdom. But as he traveled, he knew that he had met a formidable enemy who would not long remain silent.

Events similar to these must have happened in Jesus' life. He developed through boyhood to manhood in a traditional typical way. From the beginning, his love of life, for people and for story grew. He heard a special call and bravely, with difficulty, heeded it. His openness and willingness allowed a great transformation to occur in which the central message of belovedness penetrated to his depths, killing him and bringing him to a new life. Now all that had developed in him over the years was God-touched and given back to God. His storytelling, his use of his hands, his good mind and caring heart—all were given over to his mission, as we will see, were present throughout his public ministry.

It may seem that in our use of imagination to fill in the details of Jesus' early life we have taken great liberties with the Gospel evidence. However, we have only shown the obvious—that Jesus' background affected him as he entered his public ministry. In the next chapters we will see how these experiences enabled his teaching, storytelling, and power to heal.

3.

The Teaching

Like the prophets of old, certain problems awaited Jesus as he returned to society with his new message from the desert. Whenever a person makes a radical discovery about life that demands change, society rebels because it has its own ingrained patterns that tend to solidify and become rigid. It is therefore not surprising that Jesus met with difficulty and stubbornness as he preached his message. In order to be heard and comprehended, he had to devise a method that broke people free of their typical understandings about life and God. In this chapter, we will first consider several of the principal components in Jesus' teaching and how these related to his own experience of God. Then we will examine the major opponents to his message in the society and how he handled them. Finally, we will consider the primary method he used to bring his new message to life for the people.

THE MAJOR COMPONENTS

As we saw in Chapter 2, Jesus had a deeply transformative experience at his baptism that he went into the desert to understand, assess, and incorporate into the very depths of his being. A certain clarity about the factors involved in this transformation must have come to him during his desert struggle. Based on his subsequent preaching, five of these factors seem to have been particularly important to him.

Belovedness. As we have seen, the *awareness* of his belovedness to God that came to him in his baptism both affirmed the journey Jesus had taken from Nazareth and led him to contemplate his new life. Love then was the real turning point in his own process. It enabled him to face forty days in the dry and dangerous desert, to look deeply into his own soul to discover and accept the life teeming there. It also probably encouraged him to face the hard questions about what his life change meant for him. Risk surely would come with it. Rejection also was a certainty. But he must have seen that the power which equipped him to face these problems would sustain others who sought to follow his message. If he could introduce them to the love that he knew, they too would be encouraged and enabled to share with still others the message of belovedness.

Forgiveness. When the woman "who was a sinner" crashed Simon the Pharisee's dinner party (Lk 7-36–50), Jesus commented on her effusive love for him with the words "Her many sins . . . must have been forgiven her, or she would not have shown such great love" (v. 47). Jesus here drew a direct connection between forgiveness and love. Perhaps the sense of his own forgiveness had grown out of his experience of belovedness. Remember again that Jesus had left Nazareth, had broken social norms and had deserted his family. He had felt the anger, criticism, and sadness of his family and community. It would not be surprising if he had felt anger at his people in return, or if he had dwelled on this anger in the desert, complaining to God about their hardheartedness and blindness. Perhaps as he did so, God's answer became obvious. The overwhelming "I love you" from God was the vibrating answer which forged Jesus' new attitude. No matter what Jesus said or felt, God's love answered. It began to dawn on him that God's love was waiting to be met, that it answered any honest questioning with forgiveness and generosity. Thus through forgiveness, Jesus saw the love of God open up. The rich mysterious depth of love came forth as an exquisite gift that enabled Jesus to take any risk necessary to him to become more fully himself. The same process of forgiveness he later saw happening in the woman who was a sinner and as a prerequisite for others who would hear his message. **Truth.** Self-honesty was the key that opened Jesus to the full message of his belovedness. In Nazareth, on his journey, and in the desert he must have sensed in ever more powerful ways that his life as it had been was not enough to satisfy his deepest needs. Only as he admitted this and watched the intimations of God within him did he sense God's purpose for him. Had he been untrue to God's difficult call and stayed in Nazareth, he would himself never have experienced freedom and wholeness as he did. He saw that others too must be true to their inner yearnings and open to their inner fears if they would avail themselves of God's love and forgiveness.

Faith. Over and over, Jesus said to those whom he healed, "It is your faith which has healed you." Would Jesus have had such faith in faith if he had not experienced its power in his own life? It was a monumental act of faith on his part that responded to God's call to leave Nazareth. In one sense, he left everything that his life had been for nothing; no guarantees awaited him at the end of his journey. This was certainly frightening and risky for him. Others too had to face great risks if they were to follow him. They had to find a sustaining purpose to encourage them. Jesus had discovered that faith was an integral part of who he was that responded naturally and with openness to God as he let himself experience God's presence and God's love for him.

The Kingdom. Through the image of the Kingdom of heaven, Jesus brought forth his deepest understanding of God's relationship to human beings. The word kingdom was rich in its associations for his Jewish listeners. Since at least the time of King Saul, the Jewish people had striven to create an earthly kingdom under God. Periodically, as they forgot that it was God who was their true sovereign, they fell into captivity. Moses had led them forth at God's bidding from their Egyptian captivity and the Maccabees had fought to free the Jews from their captors about two centuries before the time of Jesus. About twenty-five years before Jesus began his public ministry, the Romans had conquered Palestine. Thus, as we saw in Chapter 2, the Jewish people at the time Jesus was beginning his ministry longed to be free from their present pagan captors and to re-establish their kingdom. For Jesus to speak of God's Kingdom would thus have engaged his listeners' passionate longings.

At the same time, Jesus used the image of the Kingdom in a very different sense from his contemporaries. He did not see the Kingdom as a fortified land, self-protected from all its enemies. For this reason, he eschewed the messianic expectations of the people. What he wished to express was a Kingdom of a different sort altogether. The Kingdom that he had discovered in the desert was a Kingdom of belovedness and forgiveness. It did not require political allegiance or the armaments of war. It was available to all persons who listened to the truth about themselves spoken from within them and who had faith enough to give themselves to this truth. The Kingdom manifested itself as a powerful and passionate experience of love pouring over persons and expressed itself through them to others that they too might enter into this radically different type of Kingdom.

Jesus thus used the familiar image of the Kingdom in a new way. With this image, he gained the attention of his listeners and challenged them to reconsider their basic understanding of God and of the Kingdom which they awaited. In the next chapter, we will examine in depth how Jesus used the imagery of the Kingdom to teach his listeners. But first we will consider again the society into which he brought this new and startling message of the Kingdom.

THE SOCIAL SETTING

Jesus returned from the desert into the same world that he had left. Rome still ruled Palestine, his people were still captive; nothing had really changed except for his vision of it. But Jesus saw that Rome was not the only captor; the people also were held captive by the structure of society and the rules that governed the society from within.

First century Palestine, as we saw in Chapter 2, was a structured traditional society. As in all societies, certain rules obtained and certain persons and groups exercised most of the power. Roman domination of course affected the power structure within the Jewish community. What follows is a brief synopsis of the powerful groups that Jesus confronted as he re-entered society.

The Sadducees were upper class Jews who, being politically practical, had established a working relationship with the Romans. They tried to keep the Jewish people under control in order to protect their own financially beneficial situation and to prevent a bloodbath and more restrictive domination by the Romans. The chief priests and the powerful elite of the temple in Jesus' time were Sadducees. Because of their preferred financial treatment by the Romans and their upper class status, they were generally resented by most of the Jewish population.

The Zealots were an extremist national group who hated the Romans and promulgated their violent overthrow. They were constantly trying to rouse the people to resistance and longed for a militaristic messiah who would usher in a new age. They particularly resented people who cooperated with the Romans in any way.

The Pharisees emphasized the importance of ritual purity and tithing. They were popular with the people because, unlike the Sadducees, they denied the importance of social class. At the same time, they formed a class of their own by insisting that only those who paid the required tithes and obeyed the many ritual rules of daily life were truly in relationship with God.

The Essenes were a community of believers who had left society to live in the desert in order to be able to follow God more completely and with purity. Though they didn't affect Jesus directly, he must have known of them and perhaps been in contact with them at some point during his long stay in the desert.

The Scribes held an esteemed position in society based solely on their knowledge of Scripture. Scribes were typically given a seat of honor in the synagogue and valued as the keepers of the sacred tradition. Since most sacred texts were not transmitted in written form, the primary access that the people had to an understanding of these texts was through the teachings of the scribes.

Outcasts. As we saw in Chapter 2, certain groups were considered outsiders and rejects by the Jewish society. Those who could not prove themselves to be pure-blooded Jews and those who worked certain professions such as prostitutes and tax collectors were held in low esteem. It was impossible for illegitimate Jews to ever be restored to the community. Similarly, prostitutes generally had no other financial avenues open to them and tax collectors were so disdained and resented that others tended not to want to welcome them back into the community even if they quit their offensive work. Thus, while the previously mentioned groups each held status and respect in some quarters of the population, these outcasts were rejected by one and all.

How Jesus Viewed the Situation. Jesus' teachings clearly opposed the situation just described. His values were radically different from those of the ruling class, scribes, Pharisees and Zealots. He placed so little importance on ritual cleanliness that he did not fear the presence of a prostitute or any other person who could make him ritually unclean and unable to formally practice his religion. These people were not a threat to him because ritual uncleanness could not separate him from his passionate experience of God. What did separate a person from God was what came *out* of a person's mouth from the heart. This was his angry answer to the Pharisees who wondered why his disciples did not ritually purify themselves before eating (Mk 7:5). Jesus was not against ritual per se, and probably appreciated the symbolic intent of the practice in which one made oneself ready to receive God's bounty. What annoyed him was the use of ritual to determine merit, thus making the outer form the absolute judge. Those following the form, no matter what was in their hearts, were considered justified. Such use of ritual moved the focus away from Jesus' primary concern—the person's inner spiritual condition. Jesus had frequent and particularly tumultuous encounters with the scribes and Pharisees. The scribes, who were keepers of sacred esoteric knowledge, held themselves in high esteem. That their words and decisions had binding power on people certainly supported them in this attitude. Jesus' experience of God came directly to him in baptism and in the desert; it was the intensity of this experience that had binding power for him. No words of the scribes, who were in his eyes more concerned with their own recognition than with God, could compare with the impact of God's direct presence. It did not matter to him that they had social status if their words went against his experience.

The social status of the scribes and Pharisees was important to Jesus only in that it gave them the power to convince people of their message, one that Jesus believed to be inherently wrong. Jesus' experience told him that being descendants of Abraham did not by itself guarantee salvation to the people. Rather, there was a Kingdom which had earlier been promised to Abraham that was now at hand (Gn 12:2). Accepting the Pharisees' teaching that ancestry determined merit might prevent one from entering this Kingdom. And believing that obeying ritual rules was all that was needed for salvation might draw one's attention away from the inner place where the experience of the Kingdom was found. Thus Jesus' idea of the Kingdom was in direct opposition to that of the scribes and Pharisees and threatened their status in the society. It is no wonder that some of them were from the start at enmity with him.

The Individual. Jesus' concern was for the individual, for only as an individual does one enter the Kingdom. Social recognition did not bring merit in the Kingdom. Rather, the message of the Kingdom could be put simply to each individual: "*You* matter to God. It is not important who you are or what you've been or done in your life.

If only you can believe in forgiveness and accept it, then you are close to the Kingdom."

Imagine how such words must have been received by those who were called "the excrement of the community." Take a few minutes to dwell on what it would be like to be considered the excrement of the community. You would be waste, smelly refuse; people would hold their noses around you. No one would want to be near you and you would probably be appalled and disgusted with yourself. Once you have imagined yourself in this situation, then hear the word spoken by a legitimate Israelite who because of his lineage was valued and loved within the community: "You who see yourself as excrement are much loved by God. Do not believe anyone who tells you that you have no value. Can they be right and God wrong? God knows every hair on your head, every sin about which you blush, and God forgives you and wants you to come to the feast. How can they be right to throw you out? Listen to your heart and let it cry out to God. Whatever you ask for in this way will be given you."

Jesus saw clearly that the rules of the stratified society prevented the coming of the Kingdom, that the valued and disenfranchised were prisoners alike. A society that defines certain groups as outcasts also puts great emphasis on "legitimate" people to hold to restrictive rules so that they too do not become outcasts. A breaking free from the social fabric was necessary to bring the Kingdom. This part of Jesus' teaching must have resonated with the Zealots whose primary goal was to free Israel from the Roman oppressor. But how did Jesus propose to bring about this Kingdom? His answer was the worst possible for the Zealots: "You must love your enemies." The Zealots must have grumbled: "Love the evil Romans? How? This Jesus is a dangerous madman! He is worse than the Sadducees who use the Romans to get rich, worse even than the tax collectors. *Love* the Romans, the hated enemy? Never!"

But Jesus was trying to share a deeper truth. Was not his message: "The Romans are not *the* enemy. There is some deeper hatred, some Separator bent on destroying the Kingdom. The Enemy lurks within each of us and in our midst. If you could see this Enemy, you would beat your breast, scream out in horror and plead and implore God to bring about the Kingdom now. But it is easier to hate others, to despise the Romans, the Samaritans, the whores and the dispossessed. For they are a manageable evil. They can be kept in silence and watched while the deeper wickedness goes on unnoticed. The Destroyer who convinces you that there are cases where hate is more appropriate than love manipulates and controls you. There are two great Commandments next to which all others pale. These ignored, the keeping of the others is a worthless exercise, a mound of dust and refuse. If you can love God with all that you are and bring that love to each other, you will be freed from the grip of the Enemy and will see the purpose of life, which is the opening of the Kingdom. It is for all alike, Pharisees and *pesule qahal,* scribe and unlearned peasant, man and woman, Jew and Gentile. But you cannot have what you will not allow to be. Open yourself to your enemies and you will find them inside yourself. Love your enemy and you will love yourself."

It is a painful thing to come to such an awareness of oneself, especially when one's place in society is already defined. The power of what is makes it difficult to believe in what can be. In order to reach the people, Jesus had to jar them, to shake them loose from their social bindings. To do this, his teaching and his actions had to jolt them.

A SUPRISING TEACHING

It must have been difficult for Jesus to convey what he had experienced to others. When one's experience is new and radical, it is hard for others to even *see* it. One cannot expect others to fully understand an event that radically departs from their own experience just by hearing about it. Could Jesus have walked into the villages and said: "God told me what is the truth; therefore believe me"? He needed somehow to give them a taste of the experience themselves, and he could do this only by startling them as he himself had been startled by the discoveries in the desert that had radically changed his life. Most scribes taught by taking a passage of Scripture and expanding on it, searching out its meaning and sharing it. Jesus' teaching was a radical departure from this accepted practice. He used daily situations and even events occurring at the moment in his teaching. He did this because he saw that the Kingdom was at hand in the people's very midst in the present moment. How else could he have conveyed this to people than by using daily situations? His own experience was of God's presence in his life and God's love for others. He did not come into the villages to be the incarnation of the Kingdom of God so much as to bring it about, to show each person that God was incarnate in each of them.*

Jesus' actions were part of his teachings. Not only did he utter strange teachings, he also frequently behaved in a startling and radical way. We will consider several examples of this behavior throughout the remainder of the book. Here we will take note of one situation in which he acted in a particularly shocking way to show God's love for human beings. Zacchaeus was a well-known, wealthy tax collector in Jericho (Lk 19:1–10). As Jesus passed through that town, a crowd gathered to watch him. Zacchaeus climbed into a tree so that he too might see Jesus. When Jesus saw him, he invited himself to dinner at Zacchaeus' house. Remember how hated tax collectors were and the sacredness given to sharing meals in the Middle East. By inviting himself to Zacchaeus' house, Jesus was honoring him. The townspeople and perhaps his own disciples must have been truly

---

*See e.g., Matthew 7:21 where Jesus says, "It is not those who say to me 'Lord, Lord,' who will enter the Kingdom of heaven but the person who does the will of my father in heaven"; and Matthew 6:6 where he says, "Go to your private room and when you have shut your door pray to your Father who is in that secret place. . . ."

shocked. Jesus was, through his actions, teaching everyone about the Kingdom. He obviously believed that God loved the tax collector as well as the Pharisee. If Jesus would show others the Kingdom he must act likewise. The Kingdom changed the very rules and structure of society; the Kingdom *broke* those rules which excluded persons. By this act, Jesus invited Zacchaeus back into the community and challenged the people to see how they must change if the Kingdom was to become manifest. He also risked his own credibility by making this challenge because it was fully possible that others would reject him along with Zacchaeus rather than inviting Zacchaeus back into fellowship with them.

How then would people have responded to Jesus' shocking behavior? Let us imagine for a few minutes that we are Palestinian listeners hearing several of Jesus' shocking statements for the first time. We will consider together how we might have responded to some of Jesus' strange teachings.

Jesus: In the Kingdom, the least is the greatest.

Response: *Who* could be less than a prostitute or a tax collector? Are *these* the greatest of this Kingdom?

J: John the Baptist was the greatest of men, but the least in the Kingdom is greater than John. You must be like a child to enter the Kingdom.

R: Is a prostitute greater than *John?* Can a *little child* be great?

J: The servant is the first in the Kingdom.

R: This goes too far. What *is* this Kingdom?

J: If your eye offends you pluck it out. Cut off your hand if it offends you.

R: This *healer* would have us maim ourselves rather than miss the Kingdom?

J: Give not only your cloak to the one who asks for it, but also your robe.

R: The robe too? We would be naked then!

J: If a man strikes you on the right cheek turn to him the other.

R: *That* is ridiculous! Accept a ritual insult? What would others think? Never.

J: And love your enemy . . .

These statements succeeded in shocking Jesus' listeners out of their typical view of life for a moment. Jesus sought to teach them something even more shocking. "This Kingdom that is at hand, what is it like? It's like a tiny mustard seed, but within it lives an enormous shrub. Let the tiny child who can, hear this. It is like yeast, unseen itself but the essential ingredient to bring fullness. It is like a treasure which once found surpasses all else in value, so that the person who finds it sells everything to have it . . . even if he be a Pharisee, scribe, priest or elder . . . so valuable is this treasure."

Jesus' parables and use of imagery provided a way for him to present the Kingdom, to bring the Kingdom before the people that they might find it. This very special aspect of his teaching opened the Kingdom in a radically new way to those who would see. Not surprisingly, these stories also enhance our vision of the person Jesus and his own deep spiritual experience.

4.

The Storyteller

The Gospels are full of examples of Jesus' use of imagery. Indeed, it almost seems as though Jesus spoke exclusively in images. In this chapter, we will be examining several of the sayings, parables, and stories of Jesus that exemplify his use of imagery. Before proceeding with these examples, we will first consider some of the reasons why imagery was Jesus' primary method of teaching about the coming of the Kingdom.

Because first century Palestine was an oral storytelling society, people were familiar with this method of communicating ideas. One of the highpoints of village life came when storytellers entertained the villagers with their tales. Thus, imagery was a valued and accepted part of village life.

Images and stories also serve to engage people personally, to draw them into the events being told. Unlike the legalistic teachings of the scribes and Pharisees that simply listed the rules, stories could evoke the fantasies of the Palestinian villagers. As we will see, Jesus used familiar examples from daily life in his imagery that helped involve his listeners more intimately. One reason Jesus picked these everyday images was that he believed that the Kingdom of heaven was coming into everyday life. Familiar images thus helped his listeners associate the Kingdom to their surroundings so that they might begin to sense the immediacy of God and the Kingdom.

At the same time, it is likely that many of Jesus' own insights came to him through pondering such daily images in the desert and later. In this sense, he was sharing with others his most intimate discoveries about the Kingdom when he shared these images. That he chose to return to the villages rather than remaining in the desert as John the Baptist had likewise suggests that he understood that it was primarily in daily life that the Kingdom occurred. In that sense, he was not only going back into society to share his discovery of the Kingdom; he also went to share in the Kingdom experience himself. Jesus valued the Kingdom above all else and he would certainly have wanted to experience it as deeply as possible himself. The act of sharing his insights with others thus simultaneously enhanced his own experience of the Kingdom.

As we have seen in Chapter 3, Jesus' primary concern was for the individual. The legalism of the scribes and Pharisees tended to make individuals focus on strict adherence to a set of rules. Unfortunately, legalism usually leads to rigidity and dogmatism rather than to a discovery of the Kingdom. Imagery has the power to break the hold of this outer regimentation. Jesus used images to bring individuals to a radically new understanding of themselves and their surroundings.

Imagery also serves an inner purpose. Through the imagery of dreams and fantasies, individuals can learn more about their inner condition and concerns. What is discovered there can then be used to direct one's life—in place of outer regulations. In his journey from Nazareth to the desert where he discovered the Kingdom, Jesus had himself to give up the external rules that had previously governed his life. In their place, the experience of the Kingdom provided him an internal direction. It was this that he wanted to share with others. Imagery provided for him a method of evoking the Kingdom. In fact, the very language of dreams and fantasies seems also to be the language of the Kingdom. In this sense, Jesus *had* to use images to convey his message, for logical expostulation of ideas and rules was unable to elicit the Kingdom.

When Jesus spoke in stories and images, then, his very method

was itself a potential experience of the Kingdom. He saw that everyday life was fertile soil for the Kingdom but that it was up to him to
plant the seeds of the Kingdom if it was to take hold in people's lives.
His incessant use of imagery was his attempt to sow these seeds.

IMAGES OF POWER

We will now consider several of the powerful images that Jesus
used in his day-to-day encounters with the people. As we have seen
in Chapter 3, Jesus came to the villages with a message that was antithetical to the common rules, structures and perceptions of Palestinian society. He constantly strove through his images to help
individuals understand that the way to the Kingdom demanded a
breaking away from these rules and perceptions. His own transformation had occurred within him in just this way and he knew that
any deep change in others must begin within them. But anyone who
heeded Jesus came up against the same social constraints and difficulties that he did. The power of the status quo worked against the
transformation of that person also. Indeed, the nature of Jesus' teaching so cut against traditional values that, in his own words, it "put
father against son, mother against daughter" (Lk 12:53), and those
who didn't love the message he brought more than father, mother,
family, and life itself were, he said, unworthy of the Kingdom.

Jesus further declared that he had not come to bring peace but
a sword. Out of context, this statement would have pleased the Zealots. Jesus, however, came to war not against Rome but against those
social and spiritual forces that separated people from the Kingdom.
Unless the individual cast off the old values as Jesus himself had
done, the new message would not be nourished and take hold. Thus
Jesus had to jolt his listeners with such images to shake them out of
their social trance.

Listeners must have turned shocking images like these over in
their minds, wondering what this Kingdom could be. They were

worrying too much about their lives, Jesus told them, for at the center of the Kingdom was a God who loved them. They should look at the lilies of the field, which were so beautiful without even trying, and at the birds, which without toiling were fed and taken care of. God would take care of them too and knew every little hair on their heads. God allowed the sun to shine on good and bad people alike.

Perhaps the listeners looked then toward their spiritual leaders, the scribes, and the holy men, the Pharisees, for confirmation. Should they listen to him? Did God really love bad people as well as good people? But Jesus denied the value of the opinions of the scribes and Pharisees by accusing them of separating the people from God. With his words to the scribes and Pharisees, he forced his listeners to choose between his values and the values of their spiritual leaders: "Oh you Pharisees! You clean the outside of the cup and plate, while inside yourselves you are filled with extortion and wickedness. Fools!" (Lk 11:39). "Alas for you lawyers also because you load on men burdens that are unendurable, burdens that you yourselves do not move a finger to lift" (Lk 11:46). "You blind guides! Straining out gnats and swallowing camels" (Mt 23:24).

Looking toward the scribes and Pharisees for an answer was not presented by Jesus as an option. Jesus didn't say, "Ask your holy men about me," but rather, "Your leaders are blocking the Kingdom." One isn't to mimic these leaders; one is to be like a servant or like a child. Social recognition brought one no closer to the Kingdom; it even blocked the way. The young man who could not give up his riches and follow Jesus brought forth these words from Jesus: "How hard it is for a rich man to enter the Kingdom. It is easier for a camel to pass through the eye of a needle . . ." (Lk 18:25). A rich man was considered in that society to be specially blessed by God; if he couldn't get into the Kingdom, Jesus' disciples asked, then who could be saved? Jesus' answer restated his central message about the Kingdom: "Things that are impossible for men are possible for God."

Jesus saw that it was an individual choice that opened one to the

Kingdom. Once one was open to this reality, the way was difficult and fraught with danger. "Enter by the narrow gate because the wide way leads to perdition" (Mt 7:13). Jesus seemed to be making several points with this image. One must enter by oneself through the narrow gate—a group cannot pass through it at the same time. The individual must be on the lookout even to find the narrow gate. Presumably one had to step off the wide way on which the others were traveling to go this particular way. Further, there was something to lose by choosing the wide way, for it "leads to perdition." The wide way, the way on which everyone normally travels, was thus full of danger. Jesus was warning his listeners that they were *already* on the path of danger and he wanted to shock them into getting off that path. "Many are called, but few chosen" was thus a call to awareness so that the individual would not be lulled by false guarantees that salvation would be won simply by keeping the rules.

What was the danger of the wide way? Simply that by following it people might remain forever separated from the Kingdom of God. Like the seed which contains in itself the tree, Jesus saw that persons contained in themselves an ability for deep relationship with God. Missing this relationship would be like being tied up and cast into the outer darkness where there was weeping and gnashing of teeth (Mt 25:30). To help his listeners avoid the wide way to perdition he used parables to tell them about what the Kingdom is like.

PARABLES OF THE KINGDOM

The parables of Jesus are brief "stories" which he usually used to convey his understanding of life and the Kingdom of God. As we have seen, the scribes and Pharisees had an investment in maintaining a system that gave an objective measure of personal goodness and acceptability by God. Jesus' experience of the Kingdom was just the opposite of this. It was "subjective" in that it was based on inner experience. "The Kingdom is," Jesus said, "among you and within you." It was present, immediate, able to be experienced if only the listener had ears to hear. It was "heard" in the heart and not in the head. It was for everyone, not just for those who follow specified rules. In fact, those very rule followers were blocking themselves and others from entrance into the Kingdom, and those who were unable to keep the rules actually had a better chance of finding the Kingdom: "The tax collectors and prostitutes are making it into the Kingdom before you (scribes and Pharisees) are" (Mt 21:31).

Jesus traveled the countryside teaching parables so that people might enter the Kingdom. One passage found in each of the Synoptic Gospels poses a bit of a problem in this regard. To the question "Why do you teach in parables?" Jesus is reported to have answered the following:

> The secret of the Kingdom of God is given to you, but to those who are outside everything comes in parables, so that they may see and see again, but not perceive; may hear and hear again, but not understand; otherwise they might be converted and be forgiven (Mk 4:11–12).

> The mysteries of the Kingdom of God are revealed to you; for the rest there are only parables, so that they may see but not perceive, listen but not understand (Lk 8:10).

These two parallel statements, based on Isaiah's prophecy (6:9), suggest that Jesus spoke in parables so that he might *hide* the message of God's Kingdom. Such statements are inconsistent with the personality, psychology and behavior of the man Jesus. It makes no sense that Jesus used parables primarily to hide his message. He put too much effort into presenting his message, and the parables are too rich in themselves to explain them away thus.

It is generally agreed among scholars that many statements attributed to the historical Jesus actually were visionary experiences of the early Church. At the same time, there is consensus that the parables are so individual, so specific to the unusual psychology and mentality of Jesus that they are considered genuine statements of the historical Jesus. But what are we to do with the above statements? In Matthew's version Jesus is quoted as saying:

> The reason I talk to them in parables is that they look without seeing and listen without hearing or understanding. So in their case this prophecy of Isaiah is being fulfilled:
>> You will listen and listen again, but not understand,
>> see and see again, but not perceive.
>> For the heart of this nation has grown coarse,
>> their ears are dull of hearing,
>> and they have shut their eyes,
>> for fear they should see with their eyes,
>> hear with their ears,
>> understand with their heart,
>> and be converted
>> and be healed by me (Mt 13:13–15).

Notice here Matthew's different use of the prophecy of Isaiah. Here Jesus wasn't *purposely* hiding his message from them; rather they have blinded themselves. His hope was that the parables would open their eyes and ears. Indeed Matthew later affirms this (13:34–35):

> In all this Jesus spoke to the crowds in parables; indeed, he would never speak to them except in parables. This was to fulfill the prophecy:
>> "I will speak to you in parables
>> and expound things hidden since the foundation of the world."

The immediacy and presence of the Kingdom were those "things hidden." A new vision had come into being and only through images could Jesus teach them about it. Remember that words like kingdom and messiah evoked a particular set of expectations. Imagery thus served the dual and complementary purposes of shifting emphasis away from political expectations and directly evoking this new and different Kingdom.

Jesus told no less than fifteen recorded parables about the Kingdom. In each, he used an earthy day-to-day example to teach what the Kingdom is like. Remember that Jesus' audience consisted primarily of Mideastern peasants. His choice of images was based on common knowledge and experience. What was the Kingdom like? Jesus compared it to the following: a mustard seed, yeast, a dragnet for fishing, a merchant looking for fine pearls, a pearl, a man who sowed good seed, a treasure hidden in a field, a king who was settling his accounts, a man who owned a vineyard, a king who gave a wedding feast, a man who entrusted his property to his servants, a seed which keeps on growing, bridesmaids at a wedding feast. All of these images were familiar to his listeners; each person would have visual pictures and some memories related to each image. Thus Jesus entered their past experience with these images and spoke to something they already knew.

We will now consider five of these well-known parables of the Kingdom in more detail.

The Mustard Seed

> The Kingdom of heaven is like a mustard seed which a man took and sowed in his field. It is the smallest of all the seeds, but when it has grown it is the biggest shrub of all and becomes a tree so that the birds of the air come and shelter in its branches (Mt 13:31–32).

His peasant listeners who regularly planted seeds heard in this parable that the Kingdom was available to them for the asking, as present and abundant as the multitude of mustard seeds. It was up to them to place the seed in the ground so that the life that was already there would become visible as a great shrub. Just as the peasants could count on the mustard seed to become a shrub rather than a grapevine, so too could they trust the Kingdom to come to fruition if planted in them.

In this as in many of his parables, Jesus used an earth image to express the Kingdom. He thus went against the teaching of most of the scribes and the cultural tradition that believed that God's home was in the temple. But Jesus, the man who had discovered the Kingdom in the desert, knew that God was to be found in the daily process of living.

The Yeast

> The Kingdom of heaven is like the yeast a woman took and mixed in with three measures of flour till it was leavened all through (Mt 13:33).

Again Jesus used a daily image and offended traditional sensibilities, for it was considered insulting to one's listeners in Mideastern society to mention a woman as a main character in a story. Women, as we have seen, were little valued in Palestinian society beyond their ability to bear children. In this short parable, Jesus dramatically challenged this perception of women, for here a woman was pictured as an agent of the Kingdom. Through her efforts, she enabled the yeast to leaven the flour. Life without the Kingdom, the image implies, is flat and uninteresting. And the leavening occurred through the efforts of a woman. Remember also that unleavened bread recalled the exodus of the Jews from Egypt and was prepared as part of the annual commemoration at the Passover feast, a most holy time when able-bodied male Israelites were expected if at all possible to travel to the temple in Jerusalem to celebrate. His listeners could not have failed to see the image of the leavened bread in comparison to the Passover feast. They must have asked themselves:

"Is Jesus saying that we can find God as we live our daily lives and do our work, and not only at the temple?" Jesus completely turned over the traditional values of his listeners with this simple picture.

The Treasure

> The Kingdom of heaven is like treasure hidden in a field which someone has found; he hides it again, goes off happy, sells everything he owns and buys the field (Mt 13:44).

The Kingdom could even be found in the middle of a field if one looked for it. A person must either be vigilant, energetic and thorough to find a treasure hidden in a field or else very lucky in the course of his daily work. Where the seed in the first parable was planted in the ground, this treasure was brought forth from it. There below the surface hid the great value, a treasure worth everything. His listeners, many of whom worked in the fields, probably harbored fantasies of finding such a treasure—and in a land where so many wars had been fought and spoils hidden, it was not simply an idle wish that a treasure be uncovered. Jesus used this fantasy to show where the Kingdom could be found in their own lives and that it was a joy that people would give up everything to have.

The Merchant

> Again the Kingdom of heaven is like a merchant looking for fine pearls; when he finds one of great value he goes and he sells everything he owns and buys it (Mt 13:45–46).

Here was a buyer and seller who was already looking for something of great value. What he discovered was so valuable that all his other pearls didn't equal it in worth. The Kingdom here was presented as a person looking for value. Perhaps Jesus' listeners heard in this story that the Kingdom was seeking them and thus that they were of such value that God sold all else to have them. While they sought the Kingdom it also sought them.

The Vineyard Workers

> Now the Kingdom of heaven is like a landowner going out at daybreak to hire workers for his vineyard. He made an agreement with the workers for one denarius a day, and sent them to his vineyard. Going out at about the third hour he saw others standing idle in the market place and said to them, "You go to my vineyard too and I will give you a fair wage." So they went. At about the sixth hour and again at about the ninth hour, he went out and did the same. Then at about the eleventh hour he went out and found more men standing around, and he said to them, "Why have you been standing here idle all day?" "Because no one has hired us," they answered. He said to them, "You go into my vineyard too." In the evening, the owner of the vineyard said to his bailiff, "Call the workers and pay them their wages, starting with the last arrivals and ending with the first." So those who were hired at about the eleventh hour came forward and received one denarius each. When the first came, they expected to get more, but they too received one denarius each. They took it, but grumbled at the landowner. "The men who came last," they said "have done only one hour, and you have treated them the same as us, though we have done a heavy day's work in all the heat." He answered one of them and said, "My friend, I am not being unjust to you; did we not agree on one denarius? Take your earnings and go. I choose to pay the last comer as much as I pay you. Have I no right to do what I like with my own? Why be envious because I am generous?" Thus the last will be first, and the first, last (Mt 20:1–16).

In this longer parable, Jesus compared the Kingdom to a landowner who was obviously a poor businessman. How could he expect anyone to work a full day thereafter when an hour's work produced the same reward? Jesus here took another common theme and shocked his listeners. Surely the first workers also would be given more than they expected, for such was God's generosity. But no! They were given the agreed wage. It wasn't fair. But again the Kingdom was not as they expected it to be. It couldn't be measured quantitatively; how God dealt with another person was between the two of them alone. Jesus told his listeners not to expect more because of a full day's work, for God's mercy drew tax collectors and sinners to the Kingdom as well as those who had been righteous all their lives.

Obviously, each of these parables contains many more riches than have here been discussed. I have chosen to examine several parables briefly to show how much a part of Jesus' approach were these parables of everyday life and, further, how much a part of the Kingdom he saw the daily lives of his peasant listeners to be. Jesus virtually surrounded them with examples of the presence of the Kingdom in their lives. So many familiar images disclosed the Kingdom that his listeners on hearing these stories would, as it were, have found themselves already in the Kingdom learning how to live there rather than trying to find the Kingdom so that they might enter. They were, each one of them, like the eleventh hour vineyard workers who, having only just entered the vineyard, were given almost immediately much more than they had a right to expect. The present discussion of these five parables has been an attempt to evoke that "eleventh hour" feeling, that experience of discovering that one has, against all expectations, already arrived.

STORIES OF THE KINGDOM

Frequently during his ministry when confronted with a question, Jesus would respond by telling a story. These longer stories were expressions of the same process he used in speaking in images and parables. Again Jesus chose familiar settings for his longer stories—to show his listeners that the Kingdom was a present reality and concern. Thus they were expected to give a response in the present; indeed, they were in danger of missing the Kingdom if they failed to respond. Jesus' stories set up situations for listener response and helped them see the factors involved in their choice. Usually his own choice was clear by the nature of the stories he told. The following three stories exemplify how Jesus used story to make his message known. The stories of the Samaritan, the unjust steward, and the prodigal son are chosen from the many tales Jesus told. We could, for instance, have examined a number of wedding feast stories (Mt 22:1–14; Mt 25:1–13; Lk 5:34–35; Lk 14:15–25) or stories set in the vineyard (Lk 13:6–9; Mt 20:1–16; Mt 21:28–32; Mt 21:33–46). The beauty of the stories of Jesus is that each one brings to awareness in a different way the love and forgiveness of God. Thus the three stories examined below show in essence the power, meaning, and purpose of the storytelling process used with such genius by Jesus. Several biblical critics have written extensively on these stories from many points of view. The writings of Kenneth Bailey have been particularly significant to my understanding of these stories and are consistent with the approach to the life of Jesus that I am expressing in this book.

The Samaritan

There was a lawyer who, to disconcert him, stood up and said to him, "Master, what must I do to inherit eternal life?" He said to him, "What is written in the Law? What do you read there?" He replied, "You must love the Lord your God with all your heart, with all your soul, with all your strength, and with all your mind, and your neighbor as yourself." "You have answered right," said Jesus; "do this and life is yours."

But the man was anxious to justify himself and said to Jesus, "And who is my neighbor?" Jesus replied, "A man was once on his way down from Jerusalem to Jericho and fell into the hands of brigands; they took all he had, beat him and then made off, leaving him half dead. Now a priest happened to be traveling down the same road, but when he saw the man, he passed by on the other side. In the same way a Levite who came to the place saw him, and passed by on the other side. But a Samaritan traveler who came upon him was moved with compassion when he saw him. He went up and bandaged his wounds, pouring oil and wine on them. He then lifted him on to his own mount, carried him to the inn and looked after him. Next day, he took out two denarii and handed them to the innkeeper. 'Look after him,' he said, 'and on my way back I will make good any extra expense you have.' Which of these three, do you think, proved himself a neighbor to the man who fell into the brigands' hands?" "The one who took pity on him," he replied. Jesus said to him, "Go, and do the same yourself" (Lk 10:25–37).

The context of the Samaritan story is a dialogue between Jesus and a lawyer. Indeed the story is itself part of the dialogue. At the outset, the lawyer stood and addressed Jesus as master. Typically this was the behavior of a student toward a teacher. But he questioned Jesus in order to disconcert him, not to learn, and presumably Jesus recognized this in his tone and manner. Jesus answered the question by asking the lawyer about the law, which was his area of expertise. When the lawyer responded that one must love God and neighbor, Jesus agreed with him. Had the lawyer been satisfied with the answer, no story would have been told. But having failed to justify himself in this way, the lawyer asked who his neighbor was. The lawyer no doubt felt that he knew the answer to that question too and may have hoped to say to Jesus' response that he in fact loved his neighbor. But he and the other listeners weren't prepared for Jesus' tale of a Samaritan hero.

The story begins with a man on his way down to Jericho from Jerusalem who was robbed of all he had, beaten and left half dead. This has always been a dangerous road, and those who traveled it were wary and hurried to reach their destination. First a priest happened by and passed him on the other side of the road. In those days, maintenance of the temple was an immense undertaking. Priests, Levites, and Jewish laymen, the delegation of Israel, served two week terms at the temple in Jerusalem each year. This particular priest probably had just finished his assignment and was returning home. On seeing the man he was presented with a dilemma. The likelihood was that the wounded man was a Jew but how could he know? The man was unconscious and stripped; he might even be dead. To come within four cubits of him would make the priest ritually unclean. He would thus have to return to the temple where he had just been a prominent person and stand at the Eastern Gate (where the unclean stood) in front of the altar. This was not only humiliating; the process of restoring ritual purity required that he find, buy and burn a red heifer to ashes, a ritual which took a full week. The command against defilement was unconditional for the priest while the command to love his neighbor was conditional. It was thus right for him to pass by; the legalistic system militated against his helping the wounded man.

The Levite soon came to the place and also passed by. The road between Jerusalem and Jericho curves and slopes in such a way that the Levite may have seen the priest leave the wounded man unaided. Perhaps they had served two weeks together at the temple and were both going home. The Levite on seeing the action of the priest was presented with his own dilemma. Ritual purity was imposed on Levites only in connection with cultic activities. Thus he could render aid, and the repercussions were not so serious for him as for the priest if the man were dead. But how could he, even if he wanted to, help this man whom his religious superior had avoided? No, this would be to question the integrity of the priest. Thus the Levite too left the man unaided.

The Mideastern listener would now expect a third traveler, obviously a Jewish layman, who himself had served the two weeks at the temple. But to the utter surprise and horror of the listener, Jesus replaced the expected Jewish layman with a Samaritan. As is well known, the Samaritans and Jews had a centuries-old hatred of each other. Added to that, the Samaritans had a few years before Jesus' time defiled the temple during Passover by throwing human bones into the temple court.

The hated Samaritan of Jesus' story proceeded to undo all that had been done to the injured man. Instead of passing him by, he stopped, bound his wounds, and poured oil and wine on them just as the priest and Levite had used oil and wine at the sacrificial offering at the temple. He then put the wounded man on his animal and took him to an inn. Again imagine the situation. A hated Samaritan in enemy country bringing a wounded man to an inn. A parallel modern situation might be a black man bringing a white woman who has been raped into the emergency room of a white hospital in the deep south in the 1950's. Even though innocent, he would have been treated with suspicion by most of the white people and he might even have been accused of the crime against the woman.

Such were the risks that the Samaritan took. And not only did he look after the wounded man; he promised to make good any debt the man accrued during his absence. In those days, a man who couldn't pay his debts was sent to debtor's prison. The wounded man had been robbed and had no money. The Samaritan thus took care to save him not only from his injuries but from any further debt. The Samaritan acted out of compassion for another human being, paying no heed to his own needs. It would not have been surprising for the wounded man on awakening to be angry at him, for as a Samaritan he had made the man unclean. There was a saying in those days: "Oil and wine are forbidden objects if they emanate from a Samaritan." The Samaritan thus had no hope for reimbursement, recognition or appreciation. At the same time, he was not bound by the social rules that dictated the actions of the priest and Levite (and incidentally the unseen Jewish layman). Something radical was needed to break the tyranny of these social norms. With the shocking appearance of the Samaritan doing good works Jesus attempted to do this.

After telling the story, Jesus again returned the question to the lawyer. "Which of these proved himself a neighbor to the man?"

"The one who took pity on him," was the lawyer's reply. He probably couldn't bring himself to answer simply "The Samaritan." Only then did Jesus answer the lawyer's first question, saying, in effect, "In order to inherit eternal life you must do what the Samaritan did—help your neighbor, even if he is your enemy, when he needs you."

The Kingdom of heaven occurred in the present moment when the social rules that prevented loving one's neighbor were set aside so that one could have compassion. The listener, like the priest and Levite, was presented with a choice: social acceptance in the supporting community or the freedom to reach out to one in need.

The Unjust Steward

In the following story, Jesus showed that the Kingdom could emerge in the most desperate circumstances in startling ways.

> He also said to his disciples, "There was a rich man and he had a steward who was denounced to him for being wasteful with his property. He called for the man and said, 'What is this I hear about you? Draw me up an account of your stewardship because you are not to be my steward any longer.' Then the steward said to himself, 'Now that my master is taking the stewardship from me, what am I to do? Dig? I am not strong enough. Go begging? I should be too ashamed. Ah, I know what I will do to make sure that when I am dismissed from office there will be some to welcome me into their homes.'
>
> "Then he called his master's debtors one by one. To the first he said, 'How much do you owe my master?' 'One hundred measures of oil,' was the reply. The steward said, 'Here, take your bond; sit down straightaway and write fifty.' To another he said, 'And you, sir, how much do you owe?' 'One hundred measures of wheat,' was the reply. The steward said, 'Here, take your bond and write eighty.'
>
> "The master praised the dishonest steward for his astuteness. For the children of this world are more astute in dealing with their own kind than are the children of light" (Lk 16:1–8).

This is one of the most troublesome stories in the New Testament for the modern reader. At first glance, it appears that Jesus justified the steward's dishonesty. By considering the story point by point through the eyes of Mideastern peasant listeners, a very different understanding emerges.

The story begins with the two main characters—a rich man and a steward. Most probably, the listeners assumed that the rich man was a landowner, for most rich men owned land in Palestine in those days. This steward's job was thus to make contractual arrangements between the landowner and his tenants. It had been reported to the landowner that his steward had been wasteful with his property. Perhaps he had been extorting funds or in some way cheating the landowner, but this is not stated explicitly. At any rate, the landowner confronted the steward with charges of wastefulness and, in effect, fired him.

Curiously, the steward remained silent. The Palestinian listener would have expected him to vociferously declare his innocence, blaming others, somehow trying to shift the responsibility away from himself. The landowner obviously had caught him and the steward saw the futility of proclaiming his innocence. But immediately he began to explore his options. When it became known that he had been wasteful he would not be able to get another financial position in the village. Perhaps he could dig ditches? No, he wasn't strong enough. Or beg? That would have been too embarrassing. It was a moment of crisis; what could he do?

Ah, the master was a merciful man, the steward knew, for by rights he should have been thrown into prison immediately for being wasteful and the master did not even scold him for his misdeeds. His only hope was to risk all on the mercy of his master. He still had the master's books, and for the moment no one knew he had been fired. But he must act quickly. He contacted the tenants and offered to renegotiate their contracts. Quickly he got them to write the new amount on their contracts. Were they aware of the steward's deceit? The Palestinian listener would know that they were not, for a contract revision under those terms would not be binding, but would make them partners in deception with the steward and put them in the master's bad graces. They would not do this knowingly, for they depended on use of his land for their livelihood.

Rather, the steward led them to believe that he had negotiated a better contract for them. It is likely that they had agreed to pay the landowner a set rental fee for use of his land at the time of harvest. Perhaps it had been a hard year and the expected yield was low. In such cases, the renter would normally have had to argue with the landowner for a reduction in fee. Here the master's generosity (so it appeared to them) came unsolicited.

By his actions the steward had placed his master in an awkward position. The renters would have joyfully celebrated this new arrangement. If the master had then told them the truth, they would have been furious. If, on the other hand, he let them believe that the steward had acted under his authority, he could not renege on the new arrangement. The landowner decided on the latter course and praised the steward's astuteness.

Was such dishonesty acceptable if it saved one's neck? It would have been clear to his Palestinian listeners that Jesus was not justifying the dishonesty of the steward. Rather he was praising the steward's insight into the mercifulness of the landowner and his willingness to gamble all on this mercy. Jesus was using in this story the rabbinic principle of *kal va homer*, "from the light to the heavy." If this landowner treated the wasteful steward thus, how much *more* merciful would God be to the person who risked everything on God's mercifulness?

The story thus is a metaphor of the greatness of God's mercy which, *if the person can turn to it,* will overrule the just punishment deserved by the sinner. The Kingdom of heaven then did not overlook one's shortcomings; instead it called one to account. If one could acknowledge the hopelessness of one's case if based on justice and *act* as if God's mercy would predominate, that person, like the crafty steward, would enter the Kingdom.

Notice, finally, that the behavior of the steward benefited the renters. Presumably, at the outset of the story, the steward had thought only of himself. Here his actions helped others at the *expense of the landowner*. It would be wrong to assume that the landowner did not care about his property. Only by being an astute businessman himself could he have maintained and increased his wealth. So too, Jesus inferred, was God astute in "business." The coming of the Kingdom forced the crafty steward to use his cleverness in a way that benefited others. Did not the Kingdom of heaven similarly transform the qualities of the listener who was willing to risk all on God's mercy?

The Prodigal Son and Related Parables

Jesus' genius as a storyteller is brought to fullness in the story of the prodigal son—perhaps the most famous of all his stories. It is a tale of inexhaustible content. Set in Luke 15, it is the last of three tales told to Pharisees and scribes who were complaining about how Jesus welcomed sinners and ate with them. We have already seen the emphasis placed on righteousness and ritual purity in Palestinian society. Jesus directly confronted the scribes and Pharisees in these three stories and parables, challenging them with the Kingdom of God. Before examining the story of the prodigal we will look briefly at preceding stories of the lost sheep and the lost coin.

> What man among you with a hundred sheep, losing one, would not leave the ninety-nine in the wilderness and go after the missing one till he found it? And when he found it, would he not joyfully take it on his shoulders and then, when he got home, call together his friends and neighbors? "Rejoice with me," he would say. "I have found my sheep that was lost." In the same way, I tell you, there will be more rejoicing in heaven over one repentant sinner than over ninety-nine virtuous men who have no need of repentance (Lk 15:4–7).

Jesus immediately brought his listeners into the story with his opening phrase "What man among you?" Thus he indirectly compared the scribes and Pharisees with shepherds. Though Moses had been a shepherd and God was compared to a shepherd in Psalm 23, flesh and blood shepherds belonged to a proscribed profession. Jesus was attempting to bring the scribes and Pharisees into closer contact and relationship with sinners. Certainly this comparison wasn't lost on his listeners, who were duly insulted.

In the story, Jesus pictured a shepherd who has discovered that a sheep was missing. Mideastern shepherds did not work alone. When it was discovered that a sheep was lost, one shepherd usually took the remaining sheep back to the village while the other sought out the lost sheep. Because the loss of a sheep meant hardship and loss of food and revenue for the village, the return of the lamb would have been greatly celebrated. Again we see the rabbinic principle of *kal va homer*. If a village rejoices over finding a lost sheep, how much more must God rejoice when a lost person is found!

Thus Jesus answered directly through this story the question of why he welcomed and ate with sinners—he wanted to "return" sinners to the Kingdom. The scribes and Pharisees, he implied, should have been doing the same thing. But he didn't stop there.

> Or again, what woman with ten drachmas would not, if she lost one, light a lamp and sweep out the house and search thoroughly till she found it? And then, when she had found it, call together her friends and neighbors? "Rejoice with me," she would say, "I have found the drachma I lost." In the same way, I tell you, there is rejoicing among the angels of God over one repentant sinner (Lk 15:8–10).

Jesus again shocked his listeners by making a woman the central character of the story. Notice that he did not say "which woman *among you* for, as we have seen, that would have been to his listeners an unpardonable insult and sufficient reason for them to cease listening, and besides there were no women scribes and Pharisees. That he used a woman in this story shows how far Jesus was willing to go in order that his listeners might be shocked into seeing the truth about themselves.

In this story, the woman was energetically searching for her coin. The loss of a coin would have been a tragic event because cash was in such scarce supply, and she would have turned over everything until she found it. She then celebrated with her neighbors, who would have been happy for her and delighted because the celebration would break the boredom of the repetitious days in the village. As Jesus said, "God in heaven rejoices thus over one repentant sinner." With this, Jesus compared God's actions to those of a woman, an unthinkable comparison, as we have seen, in that society.

These two parables set the scene for his tale of the prodigal. "What will he say next? To what indignity will he now subject us?" the scribes and Pharisees probably asked themselves.

He also said, "A man had two sons. The younger said to his father, 'Father, let me have the share of the estate that would come to me.' So the father divided the property between them. A few days later, the younger son got together everything he had and left for a distant country where he squandered his money on a life of debauchery.

"When he had spent it all, that country experienced a severe famine, and now he began to feel the pinch, so he hired himself out to one of the local inhabitants who put him on his farm to feed the pigs. And he would willingly have filled his belly with the husks the pigs were eating but no one offered him anything. Then he came to his senses and said, 'How many of my father's paid servants have more food than they want, and here am I dying of hunger! I will leave this place and go to my father and say: Father, I have sinned against heaven and against you; I no longer deserve to be called your son; treat me as one of your paid servants.' So he left the place and went back to his father.

"While he was still a long way off, his father saw him and was moved with pity. He ran to the boy, clasped him in his arms and kissed him tenderly. Then his son said, 'Father, I have sinned against heaven and against you. I no longer deserve to be called your son.' But the father said to his servants, 'Quick! Bring out the best robe and put it on him; put a ring on his finger and sandals on his feet. Bring the calf we have been fattening, and kill it; we are going to have a feast, a celebration, because this son of mine was dead and has come back to life; he was lost and is found.' And they began to celebrate.

"Now the elder son was out in the fields, and on his way back, as he drew near the house, he could hear music and dancing. Calling one of the servants he asked what it was all about. 'Your brother has come,' replied the servant, 'and your father has killed the calf we had fattened because he has got him back safe and sound.' He was angry then and refused to go in, and his father came out to plead with him; but he answered his father, 'Look, all these years I have slaved for you and never once disobeyed your orders, yet you never offered me so much as a kid for me to celebrate with my friends. But, for this son of yours, when he comes back after swallowing up your property—he and his women—you kill the calf we had been fattening.'

"The father said, 'My son, you are with me always and all I have is yours. But it was only right we should celebrate and rejoice, because your brother here was dead and has come to life; he was lost and is found' " (Lk 15:11–32).

In this story, Jesus set up an unbelievable situation. *No* Mideasterner would *dare* ask for his inheritance while his father was still alive, for it would be a grave insult, indeed a statement wishing the father dead. So impossible is such a request in Mideastern culture that there are no other examples of it in any of their literature. Jesus' listeners would have been shocked at the thought of it.

Another shock followed on its heels. The father agreed! The son should have been slapped, beaten to his senses, for he truly had lost his mind. The listeners must have wondered how such an unthinkable situation could arise. *No* father would *ever* agree to the request. But this father divided the property between his two sons, selling that part of his property that was the prodigal's inheritance—probably at a great loss and to his own humiliation. The son left a few days later and proceeded to squander his money.

When a famine occurred and the son found himself alone and destitute, he did the next totally unthinkable thing. He hired himself out to feed those most unclean beasts, the pigs! No more lost than this could a Jewish boy have been! Wallowing in this sty, he remembered his home and realized that the paid servants were fed while he starved. Well, he would go to his father and confess his sin and get himself hired as a servant, for he would then at least be fed.

And so he left for home. When his father saw him coming, he was moved to pity. No wonder, for his son must have been a sight!

His father's action provided the next shock to Jesus' listeners, for he lifted his skirts in a very undignified way and ran to his son. As Ben Sirach says (19:30): "A man's manner of walking tells you what he is." The listeners knew that the father was humiliating himself by doing this, and for this rascal son! Such was the father's love that he ran the gauntlet for his son. The whole village would have been furious with the son for his insulting behavior to his father. The father's kisses and embrace told them that the son was forgiven.

The father then took care to symbolically re-establish his son in the family and community. He gave him shoes to show that he was not a servant; he put his own best robe on him, acknowledging him as a most important person; and he placed on his finger what was perhaps a signet ring, thus giving him authority in family money matters. Imagine the shock of the son and the villagers. The father had acted in a totally unexpected way. So overjoyed was the father that he called a celebration announcing the return of his son, and the villagers thus were reintroduced to the prodigal in a dramatic, positive and healing way.

Such a ridiculous story! No father would accept and forgive such a son. So the listeners, the scribes and Pharisees, must have thought, and so also the elder son in the story behaved. From the beginning of the story, it is obvious that this son too was not in good relationship with his father. Mideastern protocol demanded that he intervene between his father and brother and loudly refuse his own portion of the inheritance when his brother made his request. But nothing is said in the story of his intervention, which itself indicates a separation from his father. This is confirmed later when the elder son returns from the fields. Again protocol required that he enter the party, congratulate his brother and mingle with the merry-makers. Not to do so was itself a grave insult to his father.

Again the father humiliated himself in front of the villagers by begging this son to come into the feast, for "your brother has returned safe and sound." The son answered his father harshly by proclaiming his own merit and then declaring himself a slave, not a son. No celebration has been given for him and his friends; obviously his friends were different from those present at the party. He too was separated from his father and the village.

The elder son adds a personal accusation about his brother's immorality—not stated earlier in the story—which, if true, requires death according to the law (Dt 21:18–21). But the father ignores this statement and again proclaims his love for this son, begging him to join the celebration for his returned brother.

And there the story ends! Jesus didn't tell the scribes and Pharisees what the elder son did. Clearly he did this on purpose to challenge them to decide. Would *they* come to the feast offered for the sinner? Would they like Jesus celebrate ("eat with") the sinner who returned? God, like the father in the story, rejoices when one lost is found. Jesus said, in effect, "The Kingdom is upon you! If you wish to enter the celebration you too must recognize and welcome the sinner home. All that God has is yours already. Come, celebrate the return of your brother. What are you going to do?"

In Luke 15 Jesus gave an overwhelming response to the complaint of the scribes and Pharisees. Already in the shepherd story, the point was made that God rejoices at the return of a repentant sinner. But Jesus' message was more complex than that. He was challenging his listeners, trying to involve them in the process of the Kingdom. In the stories of the shepherd and the woman, he shocked them by inferring that they were to be like shepherds themselves and that women's lives were worthy examples of the Kingdom.

Jesus must have been frustrated with the repetitious behavior of the scribes and Pharisees. When the first two stories didn't shake them loose, he told the continually shocking story of the prodigal son. After each sentence the listeners must have wondered "What next? What will he turn over now?" Then he wove his complex story, building the excitement toward a crescendo. Imagine him looking at the scribes and Pharisees, seeing that they didn't understand. If they would not be shocked *into* the story, he would leave them there so that they would have to find their way *out*. They wouldn't accept his answer, and so he told a story that would force an answer from them. Certainly he hoped they would see that they were excluding themselves from the celebration of the Kingdom. He put all of his story-telling power into the prodigal story in the hope that they would finally see.

What does Jesus' use of images in story tell us about him? Perhaps most obviously, simply that he was a brilliant storyteller and a veritable genius with images, and, further, that he was willing to risk insulting and shocking people to get them to the awareness of the Kingdom. Jesus needed story to inform his listeners of the nature of the Kingdom, for though the Kingdom is like daily life, working at the heart of daily goings-on, it is also creative, in that it seeks to bring belovedness and God's forgiveness into present awareness and experience.

In the story of the prodigal, Jesus manipulated daily images in a totally unusual way to invite his listeners to enter into an experience of the Kingdom. Jesus' own experience of the Kingdom was obviously paradoxical. God was to be found in the center of oneself in one's daily life but, once found, radically changed the face and order of that daily life.

The images of the Kingdom that Jesus used show us much more about him than just his brilliance, his courage and his desire to bring others to the Kingdom of heaven. His own experience had been in one way like the prodigal son's; he had sold everything and left home—only he was *not* accepted when he returned (Mk 6:1–6). On another level, he found a greater acceptance when he discovered that God was like the prodigal father, so great a lover that self-humiliation meant nothing compared to the return of a lost child. Jesus must have had in the desert the experience of being found by God, of an overwhelming love that embraced him and brought him into the celebration.

Or again Jesus was himself like a Samaritan in that he too did not hold the rules of Jewish society as authoritative. But he was more lonely even than the Samaritan in the midst of Jewish territory, for *no one* had yet experienced the presence and dawning of the Kingdom as he had in the desert.

Finally, the profusion of imagery that poured forth from Jesus shows how utterly "caught up" in God he was. For imagery is a picturing of the process of creation; it is in itself an act of creation. So full of creation was he that he *had to* create; he virtually burst with creativity and with the desire to bring others to the rich, full, fertile, growing life that he had discovered in himself in the middle of the parched barren desert. The imagery of Jesus tells us of his need, so like the need of the prodigal father, to take up the lost and broken child and celebrate that person's return—whether that lost person be tax collector, prostitute, dishonest steward, spendthrift son, or even a scribe or Pharisee.

5.

Healing

When John the Baptist was in prison he sent his disciples to Jesus to ask if he was "the one who is to come." Jesus is reported to have answered in this way: "Go back and tell John what you hear and see: the blind see again, and the lame walk, lepers are cleansed, and the deaf hear, and the dead are raised to life and the good news is proclaimed to the poor; and happy is the man who does not lose faith in me" (Mt 11:2–5). As this passage clearly indicates, Jesus understood his healing activity to be central to his overall mission. For many modern Christians, this proves something of an embarrassment. Since they find it so hard to believe that Jesus spontaneously and immediately cured persons, they feel that his whole ministry is thereby called into question. Perhaps it is all myth; certainly at least the reported resurrections of three dead persons must be hyperbole, for this is patently impossible. In this chapter, we will examine the healings of Jesus as an integral part of his ministry, deeply related to his teaching and storytelling. Then we will explore why, as Jesus so often stated, faith was a necessary part of the healing process. We will see how Jesus in his healing practices again went against social norms. Finally, we will examine in detail some of the healings reported to have been performed by Jesus.

HEALING AND STORY

The healing ministry of Jesus has many connections to his use of image and story. As we have just seen in the last chapter, Jesus used stories to bring the Kingdom of heaven into focus for his listeners. This Kingdom did not require that a person be of upright moral character. Rather, crooked stewards, hated Samaritans, and squandering sons were all welcome there. Their decision to trust everything to God, to act in new ways, was the crucial element. So too in healing, as we will examine below, the primary ingredient was expectant trust. Apparently, one could neither be healed nor enter the Kingdom without this trust. In fact, the healing done by Jesus can be understood as an outpicturing of the Kingdom. Just as imagery helped his listeners perceive the possibility of the Kingdom, healing was an outer manifestation of it.

Modern medicine has described a connection between imagery and healing. Physiologically, the autonomic (or "unconscious") nervous system, which among other things regulates heart rate, circulation, digestion, and responses to tension, speaks and understands the language of images. The peripheral nervous system, on the other hand, understands verbal commands. Try this simple experiment. Use words to tell your right hand to touch your head. It is easy to follow that command providing you have no nerve or muscular damage. Next tell your mouth to salivate. Probably you will not succeed. Now imagine your favorite food. In your mind's eye smell its aroma, look at it, see yourself putting the first delicious bite of it in your mouth. You will probably find yourself beginning to salivate. This response is under autonomic control and responds to pictures and images. There appears to be a relation between the prefrontal lobe of the brain which deals with images, the hypothalamus, and healing. It has been hypothesized that when positive images are created in the prefrontal lobe, these are communicated to the hypothalamus which then informs the endocrine and immune systems and enables them to assist healing. It has also been hypothesized that negative energy is communicated to the body in the same way, with negative results. Thus, the theory goes, positive imagery benefits the health of the individual.

Jesus used such imagery to bring his listeners into relationship with the creative center of life. In his stories, he pictured this center as being like a loving father who willingly humiliated himself to guarantee his son's safety, as a just but deeply merciful landowner, and as a rejected but loving Samaritan who risked his own safety because he was moved to compassion by the suffering of a fellow human being. Jesus' own behavior was consistent with his stories. He like the prodigal father feasted with the lost son (e.g., tax collectors and sinners) who had returned, and like the Samaritan he responded to the suffering of others by bringing healing.

Like his stories, Jesus' healings went against the prevailing beliefs and customs, for the Deuteronomic view held that all illness was caused by God and was most probably related to the sins of the person and/or his or her ancestors. The Pharisees believed in this view of illness and in fact accused Jesus of being in league with the devil. For wasn't he going against God's wishes by healing the sinner? Jesus answered this charge with an image: "Every kingdom divided against itself is headed for ruin" (Mt 12:25). His view was that illness is caused by some negative reality which is opposed to the Kingdom. God didn't want people to be sick, for illness made it more difficult for people to relate to God. Only by turning toward the Kingdom could one escape this destructive force.

Jesus used parables and images to shock his listeners into perceiving the Kingdom, to create in his listeners what modern researchers call an "altered state of consciousness." When people were jolted out of their normal view, they had the opportunity to perceive a new and different level of reality (the Kingdom) which operated under different rules than "normal" reality. Just so did healing affect the crowds. They were "amazed," "in awe," "frightened" by his power, and once Jesus was asked to leave town because he so intimidated the people by his healing power (Lk 8:26–39). Thus, healing was both an outer manifestation of the Kingdom that shocked people out of their normal ordered perception of life and a way of opening people to the Kingdom.

Jesus wasn't only attempting to make available entry into the Kingdom; he also sought to *bring* the Kingdom into outer reality, into daily life. Healing was one means of accomplishing what his stories suggested, that the love of God is not only forgiving but healing, that God doesn't see goodness in the traditional sense of following rules but as relationship with individuals which is by its very nature healing. In this sense, Jesus couldn't help but heal; it happened naturally as part of the incarnation of the Kingdom in everyday life.

In several places throughout the Gospels, we read that Jesus told those who were healed to be silent about the healing, to tell no one. On the surface, this seems a strange and impossible request. How is the leper or the blind man or the lame person supposed to keep secret the dramatic change which had occurred from those who have long known him? Perhaps by considering the central message of Jesus' teaching we will find a key to understanding Jesus' words. If the Kingdom was primary, Jesus himself needed to stay "out of the way." The all too human tendency is to adulate the one who does the special deed, in this case healing. It was more important to Jesus that the Kingdom of heaven be recognized than that he himself be honored. The longing for a Messiah among the Jews may have led people to put Jesus before his message. But Jesus was no magician. His ability to heal was in part determined by the faith of the person seeking healing. Did Jesus want people to understand that the importance of what had taken place was not that *he* had healed but that the person had come into contact with the Kingdom?

FAITH AND HEALING

In a great number of the healing stories, Jesus said to the person who had been healed something like this: "Go your way; your faith has healed you." He did not take direct credit himself for the healing. But what did he mean when he said that people's own faith was what had saved them?

As we have seen, it is in the nature of the Kingdom that healings occur. Jesus' main goal was to make manifest this Kingdom. Through images, stories, his behavior and healing, he sought to demonstrate the power of the Kingdom. Clearly he himself had a strong faith in God which was clear to his listeners. His desert experience had taught him that he could trust God above all things. This experience *was* faith; he could not have come to know the Kingdom if he did not have this trust.

This is the tricky thing about the Kingdom; it isn't something which can be understood by rational argument. Rather a shift in awareness, a new experience, is needed, and when it happens, one "knows" that the power and love are there. In one situation where the Apostles were unable to heal an epileptic, Jesus told them that they had failed because they had little faith. He went on to say: "If your faith were the size of a mustard seed you could say to this mountain, 'Move from here to there,' and it would move; nothing would be impossible for you" (Mt 17:20). Notice three things in his answer. First, he used a shocking image, a *tiny* seed capable of moving a *huge* mountain. He was again trying to shift them into a different awareness. Second, faith is not quantitative; rather it is a qualitative experience. One has it or one doesn't. Third, to have it gives one an almost unbelievable source of power.

Thus Jesus' great faith shone through his stories, actions, and person and quickened the faith of those around him. This was particularly important in cases of illness because illness itself usually has a negative impact on the faith of the sufferer. At the point a person *most* needs faith, most needs positive expectancy, just then is it most difficult to harness that faith. Something about Jesus inspired sick people in a dramatic way so that the "impossible" could occur. If the Gospels are to be believed, Jesus was surrounded by a virtual explosion of healings. Among the forty-one different cases of healing cited,

nineteen accounts of healings of the multitudes are given. In themselves, these healings would have reinforced Jesus' own faith in the
power of the Kingdom. In fact, Mark (6:1–6) reports that Jesus was
shocked by the lack of faith of his own townspeople and that he could
work no miracle there though he cured a few sick people on the out-
skirts of town. Seemingly, there was a certain type of faith from others that he could regularly count on which enabled him to heal.
When that faith was lacking, he was powerless to effect healing. It
was indeed the person's faith in the Kingdom which itself was manifested in the person Jesus that brought about healing, not Jesus
alone.

THE SOCIAL SITUATION

We have already been introduced to the cast of characters in Jesus' world. Earlier, we examined how Jesus used stories and images
in his attempt to break Pharisee, scribe and peasant away from their
overly ritualized rule-bound behavior and understanding. Not surprisingly, Jesus also used healing in his attempt to break the stran-
glehold of tradition. He did this in three ways: by healing on the
sabbath, by separating illness from its absolute connection with sin,
and by healing Gentiles.

Healing on the Sabbath

There are at least six separate accounts in the Gospels of Jesus
healing on the sabbath. Three of these healings took place in the synagogue where devout Jews gathered on the sabbath to hear the word
of God. Jesus must have made a conscious decision to heal in the synagogue, for he knew that his actions would enrage the scribes and
Pharisees. In the first account in Mark (1:21–28), Jesus cast a demon
out of a man and the "people were astonished" and "his reputation
rapidly spread everywhere." Surely, this annoyed the scribes and
Pharisees who saw him as a threat to their way of life. Mark's second

account of a sabbath healing also takes place in the synagogue (3:1–6). In this case, a man was there who had a withered hand and they were watching Jesus "to see if he would cure on the sabbath day, hoping for something to use against him." After ordering the man to stand in the middle of them, Jesus asked if it was against the law on the sabbath to do good or evil; to save life or kill. But they didn't answer him. Thereupon, angry at them, he healed the man and the Pharisees began to discuss how to destroy him.

As we have seen, one of Jesus' ongoing problems was his inability to jolt the Pharisees and scribes out of their obstinate position. He succeeded only in angering them because his behavior broke the rules of their tradition. Jesus healed on the sabbath because he hoped that by bringing the fruits of the Kingdom into juxtaposition with ritualized behavior, it would become obvious to the scribes and Pharisees which was the right course. For it was obvious to Jesus that to cure a person was immensely more important than to follow protocol. If a conflict existed between rules and a person's welfare, the course of action was clear. At times, Jesus appeared to be dumbfounded by their hardheartedness. After healing a man with dropsy (edema) on the sabbath, he asked the Pharisees, "Which of you here, if his son falls into a well, or his ox, will not pull him out on a sabbath day without hesitation?" (Lk 14:5).

Separating Sin and Illness

Jesus also broke with the typical view in his hatred of illness and in his belief that illness did not come from God. He understood that illness made people more vulnerable to despair—particularly in a society which saw illness as the effect of sin. By rebelling against the Deuteronomic notion that all illness resulted from sin, Jesus helped free sick people so that they might have the faith that would heal them. Like the members of despised professions, people with illnesses were often looked down upon as sinners. Thus, illness by the society's definition put the person outside the pale of God's mercy.

The sick person had not only to get well but to "make things right with God." This is a heavy burden for anyone, but particularly for one who is ill. Sick people must have felt the judgment of their community; indeed they were like scapegoats—those who were healthy could look at them and think: "If that person's illness shows God's displeasure, then I who am well am in God's favor."

Jesus saw that this attitude was incorrect for a number of reasons. First, the sick person needed compassion to get well, for judgment stimulated negative images which worked negatively on the body. Second, the sick person was separated from the community and forced to do battle alone. If, as Jesus thought, the battle was against forces of evil which sought to destroy, then communal protection and positive attitudes were imperative to aid the ill person. Third, the Kingdom was available to the person who had faith. It was next to impossible for a sick person to have expectant trust given the prevailing attitude and tradition. Fourth, Jesus didn't believe in the absolute relationship between sin and illness. In fact, the belief in this absolute connection was destroying people. Fifth, this attitude also kept those who were judging the sick out of the Kingdom, because they too were caught in a negative expectation. Only as they obeyed every rule were *they* acceptable to God—and if they broke the rules, God might make them sick. This untenable position made it impossible for them to let go of the rules which held them and thus blocked them from seeing that God, like the loving prodigal father, already forgave any sins and welcomed them home. Not knowing that they were out of relationship to God, they did not seek to re-establish this relationship.

Healing Gentiles

The third way Jesus broke the social norm was by healing Gentiles. In the two examples noted in the Gospels, Jesus was impressed by the faith of the Gentile petitioners. In the first case (Mk 7:24–30), a Syro-phoenician woman begged Jesus to cure her daughter. When he retorted that he had come for the lost sheep of Israel and that the dogs (pagans) shouldn't get the children's (Israelites') food, she answered that even the dogs could eat the scraps which fall from the table. Jesus was impressed by her answer and submitted to her pleas. What in particular impressed him? Pagans knew that the Jews had no use for them and considered them unclean. It took tremendous faith for this pagan woman to break through these barriers and beg for mercy from a Jew.

In the second story (Mt 8:5–13), a centurion came to Jesus to beg for healing for his servant. When Jesus agreed to come and cure him, the centurion declared himself unworthy and asked only that the word be given. As a man under authority himself, he knew that he could trust orders to be carried out. Just as his men were subject to him, he saw that the spirits of illness were subject to Jesus. Not his presence, but only a *word* was necessary to bring healing. Jesus was *astonished* and said that he had seen nothing like this in all of Israel. Clearly this man already had a sense of the Kingdom.

Perhaps Jesus learned something from these two pagans. The woman's fortitude and the man's trust were greater than he had seen among his own people. At the least they affirmed his own experience of the Kingdom. His willingness to encounter them and to grant their requests shows dramatically that he believed that God was working in a different way than the Israelites thought. Their rejection of the Gentiles actually *blocked* God's attempt to work among them. The Kingdom of heaven found all those who had faith in it. Rules didn't matter; genealogy didn't matter; sex didn't matter; social title didn't matter; nor did adherence to social norms. Only faith and love mattered.

TYPES OF HEALING

To gain a deeper understanding of Jesus' healings and how they relate to the Kingdom, we will now examine three types of healings:

(1) healings among the crowds, (2) healings of demoniacs, and (3) physical healings. We will use imaginative stories to enter more deeply into each type of situation in which healing occurred.

THE CROWDS

We have already noted that nineteen of the forty-one physical and mental healings reported in the Gospels—nearly half the examples—summarize healings of large numbers of people. These general accounts should be examined if we want an overall picture of Jesus' healings. We will now look at several of these reports.

That evening they brought him many who were possessed by devils. He cast out the spirits with a word and cured all who were sick (Mt 8:16).

And he asked his disciples to have a boat ready for him because of the crowd, to keep him from being crushed. For he had cured so many that all who were afflicted in any way were crowding forward to touch him (Mk 3:9–10).

People recognized him . . . and brought the sick on stretchers to wherever they heard he was. And wherever he went, to village, or town, or farm, they laid down the sick in the open spaces, begging him to let them touch even the fringe of his cloak. And all those who touched him were cured (Mk 6:55).

He was with a great crowd of people from all parts of Judea and from Jerusalem and from the coastal region of Tyre and Sidon who had come to hear him and to be cured of their diseases. People tormented by unclean spirits were also cured, and everyone in the crowd was trying to touch him because power came out of him that cured them all (Lk 6:17–19).

Let your imagination create a picture of what these accounts imply. Picture a possible situation.

Late in the afternoon, word passes through your village that Jesus of Nazareth and his disciples have left a nearby village after preaching and healing there all day. They have set up camp in the hills just outside your own village. Your heart is pounding and you feel a surge of energy. Perhaps if you leave now you can take your daughter out to him. You know his reputation as a great healer. His works have already become part of the village folklore. Old Aaron had one time suggested taking little Ruth to him. Perhaps Jesus could do something for her stomach pains. Something has to be done soon for the whole village has grown impatient with her screaming. And it's so unpredictable; she is fine for several days and then her appetite disappears and holding her belly she cries out in anguish. Neither medicine nor prayers have helped. Her brothers and sisters are embarrassed by her outbursts. It seems that if nothing is done, the family will soon dissolve. Maybe if you get her to Jesus he can help her. Ruth is alone in the dark of the house—caught in one of her attacks. With her brother Simon's help, you could probably carry her out to the hills. It shouldn't be too difficult because Ruth is now light as a hen's tail although her struggling and groaning might make it more difficult to balance the stretcher. Under protest, Simon agrees to help you. He is tired of his sister's sickness and of the villagers' complaints. Together you place Ruth on the stretcher and carry her outside. Mercifully, she is exhausted and she cooperates by lying still as a corpse during your journey to the hills. Already you sense the excitement of the village. Others are hurrying in the same direction. Some are carrying and supporting their old and infirm. Your heart sinks. You'll never even get close to Jesus. You hear the laughter and excitement of your friends and then you look at Ruth. Her face is drawn and gaunt. Her eyes stare vacantly into yours. You urge Simon to hurry and you pass many others as you practically run to where Jesus is claimed to be. Finally, you see him. He has come out of the hills and stands in a pasture at the foot of the hills. He is surrounded by people. As you get closer, you hear groans and crying, laughter, shouts of joy. Someone from another village runs up to you, beaming, with tears rolling down his cheeks. "Hurry! Hurry!

Your girl will be healed. Yahweh be praised! My mother walks—after ten years!" he shouts and runs to tell others. Your heart leaps into your throat. Perhaps, perhaps. Even Simon seems excited. Before long, you are surrounded by a sea of healed humanity. Ruth is being jostled by the crowd and she cries out as she grabs her belly. Suddenly you are standing next to Jesus. With a look of sadness he touches Ruth's cheek, strokes it. Ruth is grimacing, seemingly in more pain. Not there, you want to shout. Can't you see? It's her stomach. Jesus turns to you, speaks, asking a strange question. "Who is it that has died?" Died? No one, no one! No one but . . .

"Her friend died after she mistakenly ate a poisonous plant," you tell him. "She is grieving the loss of her friend," Jesus says. He takes Ruth's hands and lifts her to her feet and embraces her, holding her for a long time. A hush has fallen over the crowd. An old woman cackles, "See, he is about to heal her." Then Jesus makes Ruth lie down on the ground and touches her stomach with both hands. "Grieve no more, my little friend. Esther is happy now and prepares a place for you," he says. Ruth sits up suddenly. For the first time in ages, in fact, since Esther's sudden death, she smiles. It is as though a glow of healing spreads from her mouth to her whole face. The crowd senses that a healing has occurred and cheers. You know that Ruth will now be well.

What modern science calls the placebo effect was at work among these crowds; the positive expectation of healing was healing in itself. At the same time, so great was the collective belief of the crowds in the power of Jesus that they might have inadvertently crushed him in their desire to touch him—something of a "snowball effect" of positive expectancy. The healing power of Jesus elicited more faith. Jesus became not only the bringer of the Kingdom but its focus. His person was for the crowds the embodiment of power, and thus they needed to touch him to reach that power. Their faith may not compare to that of the centurion who so recognized Jesus' authority that he asked only for the word to be given; however, we must not diminish the great faith born of need and suffering which the crowds exhibited, for they were able to recognize the healing power coming through Jesus and thus be open to it. Compare this to Jesus' visit among his own townspeople in Nazareth (Mk 6:1–6). They saw him as a carpenter and would not accept him as anything else. They knew so well what he had been that they couldn't see what he had become. Their negative expectations prevented him from working any miracle there and he cured only a few people. Thus we see the importance of positive expectancy for healing to occur. No wonder Jesus so often told people that it was their faith that saved them. He needed that faith if the healing was to happen.

DEMONS

Perhaps the story of the epileptic boy who was brought by his father to Jesus for healing is the best known account of Jesus casting out a possessing spirit. We will use Mark's version (9:14–29) of this healing in the following imaginative exercise. The story is told here using the father's voice.

What hope can there be for us now? I've made the long trip with Malachi and nothing has happened. Everything I owned is gone. It has been going on now for fifteen years. He would be better off dead, I think. Even these men haven't helped him. How frustrated they are. Look at him squirming on the ground, writhing, slobbering. They fully expected to heal him. But he is beyond healing. And where is their leader, this great man Jesus, who supposedly works such cures? Someone said he is up in the mountains with three of his men. These men here, they are his followers. They use his name for healing. Most of the other afflicted people have been healed. Oh this is too horrible! We are cursed by God! Even healers cannot heal him! God, let him die! Let me die!

His disciples seem angry. The crowd is growing agitated.

Several suggestions are being shouted to them.

A crippled man is speaking, "Get that boy away. He will prevent healing for the rest of us."

Words of agreement come from the crowd. I'm afraid they will turn on us soon. Malachi feels their anger. Don't they see that he understands them? It will just make him worse.

Wait, what is it they're saying? Jesus is here! The crowd parts to let him pass. His disciples are bringing him toward us. Look, he is angry. There is fire in his eyes as he looks at the crowd. Oh please, don't hurt Malachi!

He speaks to the disciples. His voice is harsh: "What are you arguing about with them?"

I must say something or he will hurt him. Look at his power.

"Master, I have brought my son to you; there is a spirit of dumbness in him, and when it takes hold of him it throws him to the ground, and he foams at the mouth and grinds his teeth and goes rigid. And I asked your disciples to cast it out and they were unable to."

With fierceness he turns from me to his followers: "You faithless generation. How much longer must I be with you? Bring him to me."

They bring my boy out of the crowd from behind me. Another fit seizes him. He falls to the ground, writhing, moaning. Oh do something please! Malachi!

"How long has this been happening to him?"

"From childhood, and it has often thrown him into the fire and into the water in order to destroy him. But if you can do *anything* have pity on us and save us."

His anger then turns to me: "If you can? Everything is possible for anyone who has faith."

Faith? Why do you think I brought him this great distance? But your disciples have failed. "I *do* have faith. Help the little I have!"

The crowds are pressing closer. They will trample us. Do something!

Jesus looks at the crowd and then, taking a deep breath,

says quietly with grim determination, "Deaf and dumb spirit, I
command you: come out of him and never enter him again."
        Aiee! Malachi! It is killing you, tearing its way out of you!
Malachi! Are you—is he dead?
        Jesus is grabbing his hand, pulling him up. Malachi is
looking at me. He opens his mouth, "Daddy, daddy! It has
gone! It is gone!"
        "Malachi, you are all right! It is gone! Malachi!"

If a general discussion of the possibility of faith healing makes
the modern reader edgy, the specific area of demonology will probably induce mild hysteria or shocked skepticism. Three things should
be kept in mind when examining these accounts. First, most modern
thought has debunked belief in demons as primitive superstition.
One introductory psychology textbook describes the medieval practice of boring holes in the person's head to release demons as an example of the barbarian superstition above which modern thought has
risen. Jesus' view of demons was more sophisticated than this. His
experience taught him that God wanted persons to enter the Kingdom. Negative beings or spirits bent on preventing this and on destroying the individual sometimes took hold of a person so that entry
into the Kingdom was impossible. These negative spirits brought
about dumbness, deafness, blindness, thrashing about or "epilepsy,"
general lack of control and violence. None of these conditions are unknown to modern psychiatry. Catatonic stupor and spontaneous violent outbreaks both are all too well-known modern experiences.
Seemingly, similar experiences to what Jesus knew as "demons" are
known to modern psychiatry under different names such as hysterical
reaction, catatonia, and other forms of schizophrenia.
        Second, the language and world view of the time understood
these occurrences to be manifestations of demon possession. As a
member of that culture, Jesus shared this view. It is important to realize that terms of schizophrenia and hysterical reaction would have
been as meaningless to them as the notion of demon possession is to

many of us. There could have been no expectant trust or healing if
they did not share a common view of what was the cause of the problem. Third and most importantly, Jesus' method *worked*. He was able
by recognizing the problem as demon possession to effect an immediate cure, something that modern psychiatry has usually failed to
do. It was Jesus' working hypothesis that spirits could enter and
sometimes overtake individuals. By treating people in this way, he
was able to cure them—which supported his working hypothesis.
Further, Jesus didn't identify every situation as possession. There
were discrete markers, as we saw above, that signaled possession. I
personally believe that his working hypothesis was a beneficial approach for him to take in his healing work.

We will now look at two other cures of reported demon possession.

The Dumb Spirit

> They had only just left when a man was brought to him, a dumb
> demoniac. And when the devil was cast out, the dumb man
> spoke and the people were amazed. "Nothing like this has ever
> been seen in Israel," they said. But the Pharisees said, "It is
> through the prince of devils that he casts out devils" (Mt 9:32–
> 34).

Several things are worth noting in this story. First of all, the
crowd knew the man as a dumb demoniac. For whatever reasons, he
could not speak and they had been unable to help him. Obviously,
to them, a demon prevented his speaking. Second, *something* happened between him and Jesus which changed the situation. Perhaps
the man saw in Jesus someone stronger than whatever kept him
dumb. This then inspired faith in him and broke the hold of the
dumb spirit. Third, the crowd's amazement shows that they didn't

fully believe the man could be helped, but they interpreted the outcome positively. Finally, the Pharisees who saw the same thing interpreted it negatively. Only one in league with devils could coax them out. They didn't deny that the healing had occurred; rather, they *interpreted* it differently. Jesus was seen as having power but from a different source than God.

The Gerasene

They came to land in the country of the Gerasenes, which is opposite Galilee. He was stepping ashore when a man from the town who was possessed by devils came toward him; for a long time the man had worn no clothes, nor did he live in a house, but in the tombs. Catching sight of Jesus he gave a shout, fell at his feet and cried out at the top of his voice, "What do you want with me, Jesus, Son of the Most High God? I implore you, do not torture me." For Jesus had been telling the unclean spirit to come out of the man. It was a devil that had seized on him a great many times, and then they used to secure him with chains and fetters to restrain him, but he would always break the fastenings, and the devil would drive him out into the wilds. "What is your name?" Jesus asked. "Legion," he said, because many devils had gone into him. And these pleaded with him not to order them to depart into the abyss.

Now there was a large herd of pigs feeding there on the mountain, and the devils pleaded with him to let them go into these. So he gave them leave. The devils came out of the man and went into the pigs, and the herd charged down the cliff into the lake and was drowned.

When the swineherds saw what had happened they ran off and told their story in the town and in the country around about; and the people went out to see what had happened. When they came to Jesus they found the man from whom the devils had gone out sitting at the feet of Jesus, clothed and in his full senses; and they were afraid. Those who had witnessed it told them how the man who had been possessed came to be healed. The en-

tire population of the Gerasene territory was in a state of panic
and asked Jesus to leave them. So he got into the boat and went
back.

The man from whom the devils had gone out asked to be
allowed to stay with him, but he sent him away. "Go back
home," he said, "and report all that God has done for you." So
the man went off and spread throughout the town all that Jesus
had done for him (Lk 8:26–39).

Let us again use our imaginations to enter the story. Perhaps in
your own life you have been approached, passed, or attacked by a violent frightening person. In your mind's eye, picture what that person looked like (or would look like if you fortunately haven't had such
an encounter). Perhaps you envision a large man, with wild eyes,
gritted teeth, disheveled hair, tense shoulders, arms out from his
body with fists clenched, crouching and ready for attack, screaming
wild obscene phrases. Even picturing such a person in your mind may
make your heart beat faster. In this story, Jesus confronted a man near
the tombs who so frightened the townspeople that he had been forced
out of town. Imagine a naked wild man coming toward you and
throwing himself at your feet while you walked through a cemetery.
The very thought of it may send chills up your spine.

The ensuing dialogue indicates that the demon recognized Jesus, who on seeing the man had been praying that the demon would
leave him. Jesus' first response to the demon possession was to pray
in order to expel the demon, and this led the demon to beg Jesus not
to torture it. This suggests that the demon saw Jesus' power and was
afraid of him. The reader may have noticed that the demon's name—
Legion—has obvious political overtones, for it was the Roman legion
that kept the Israelites tormented in chains. Sending the demon into
the unclean pigs, into animals considered untouchable by the Jews,
symbolically dispensed with the Romans and sent them charging
down the hill to their destruction.

How are we to understand this story? Is it purely metaphori-

cal—expressing the desire of the Gospel writers and early Jewish
Christians to see the Romans crushed? Is it purely factual? Did the
demon in fact answer as reported? If so, what did this answer mean?
Perhaps this wild man was possessed and had lost his mind because
he saw clearly how enslaved were his people. His ravings would have
deeply upset the other villagers who did not wish to see so clearly how
truly enslaved they were by Rome and so they banished him from
their midst, seeking, at the same time, to banish their own awareness
of their plight. Neither of these options seems improbable. Personally, I think that there is a combination of fact and metaphor in this
story. As stated earlier, Jesus was successful in many other situations
in relieving people of spirit possession. Perhaps in this story a true
healing occurred that later had attached to it a political message. Perhaps the political situation in itself contributed to the man's possession. Either way, a powerful transformation occurred when the man
met Jesus.

The specific situation, however, had other than political importance. When the townspeople saw that the man had come to his
full senses, they panicked and asked Jesus to leave them. His power
was too much for them. They somehow felt safer sending the man to
the tombs than believing that a greater power than "Legion" could
exist. The account tells us that Jesus simply obliged them, got into
his boat and left.

Notice in this situation that the demoniac exhibited no expectant faith and yet Jesus was able to heal him. This may have been possible for two reasons. First, the "negative faith" of the townspeople
was not present out in the lonely graveyard. Second, Jesus himself
acted as the person with faith for the demoniac, as had the Syro-
phoenician woman for her daughter and the centurion for his servant.

What do these stories of possession tell us? First, the "demons"
exerted a powerful effect on people. It was particularly hard for them
to believe that demons could be overcome. When they were overcome there was a feeling of awe and sometimes even panic because a
power greater than the demons had been demonstrated. Abused by

power as they had been, it must have been hard for them to trust the good will of any such power. Jesus, on the other hand, saw this power as a manifestation of the Kingdom, where they were full citizens, loved, valued and cared for.

Second, the negative beliefs of the crowds made it imperative for Jesus to be the one with expectant faith. In the story of the boy, a weak and pleading faith (the father's) was expressed. In the story of the Gerasene demoniac, no positive faith at all was shown. Healing of "demon possession" was primarily of the intercessory type. In cases where no one else had enough faith, Jesus' own belief brought about the healing. So against the destructive effects of the evil forces was he that he prayed that this evil be overcome. This suggests that he was in an ongoing relationship with God, praying that the negative forces be defeated, and imagining the victory of the Kingdom which he had already experienced.

PHYSICAL HEALINGS

Several examples of Jesus healing physical illness are recorded in the Gospels. We will begin our consideration of this type of healing by imagining ourselves as the blind beggar in Jericho as he hears that Jesus will soon be passing by (Lk 18:35–43).

> "Alms for the poor, alms for the blind!"
> Well it is a living for a blind man. Crowds of people rush to Jerusalem to share the Passover with their families. Ah families. Six years now, I am blind. I cannot take care of my children. Their uncles have to do that. I bring home only a pittance.
> "Alms! Alms! Gifts for God's poor!"
> I spent many Passovers in Jerusalem. I worshiped God with my own offerings. But now—never again will I see God's holy place. Never again will I look into little Jonathan's eyes. My pride, my son!
> "Alms!"

Jonathan. His eyes sparkled so when I played with him. Now my eyes are dead!

"Alms! Have mercy on me!"

I want to see my boy again.

"Alms!"

Someone pushes me. "Get back, you. A large crowd is coming. Jesus from Nazareth and his followers are going to Jerusalem."

"The healer? Jesus?"

"The same. Maybe he will heal you, blind man. Now get back, make room!"

Heal me? Heal me? Give me my sight? I could see Jonathan! Jonathan!

"Jesus!"

"Shut up, you! We won't hear what he has to say if you're screaming. Shut up!"

"JESUS!"

"Silence, man!"

Someone slaps me.

"Jesus, son of David, have mercy on me!"

"Get him out of here."

"HAVE MERCY!"

Silence. The crowds have stopped walking. What is happening? Someone lifts me from my knees.

"What are you doing?"

"You have your wish, beggar. He will see you."

A gentle voice filters through the silence. The words touch me like sight. Already in that tone I can hear my sight. I'm going to see! Oh! Jonathan!

"What do you want me to do for you?" he asks.

It is already happening. I can feel my tears cleansing my eyes, washing away my blindness. I am going to see Jonathan. I haven't seen him for six years. "Sir, sir!" I can't stop crying and shaking. "Sir, let me see again."

The mystery of God fills me. It is as if I stand in the Holy of Holies. I alone am allowed to behold the sight. Only one who hasn't seen can know. Jesus! Jonathan!

His gentle hands touch my eyes.
"Receive your sight. Your faith has saved you."
Opening my eyes, I see him. Clearly. I can see a human
face. There are his eyes, his nose. I am seeing his beard as I stroke
his cheek. He is smiling. I have seen no smile for years. It is the
Holy of Holies! My blindness is now from tears of joy.
"Yahweh! Hosanna! Praise, praise God! Jonathan!"

Physical illness bothered Jesus as much as did mental and spiritual illness and his response to it was the same. He saw that it too
separated people from God and burdened them. His compassion led
him to relieve these suffering people also. We will now look closely
at two accounts of physical healing.

Ten Lepers

Now on the way to Jerusalem he traveled along the border between Samaria and Galilee. As he entered one of the villages, ten
lepers came to meet him. They stood some way off and called to
him, "Jesus! Master! Take pity on us." When he saw them he
said, "Go and show yourselves to the priests." Now as they were
going away they were cleansed. Finding himself cured, one of
them turned back praising God at the top of his voice and threw
himself at the feet of Jesus and thanked him. The man was a Samaritan. This made Jesus say, "Were not all ten made clean?
The other nine, where are they? It seems that no one has come
back to give praise to God, except this foreigner." And he said
to the man, "Stand up and go on your way. Your faith has saved
you" (Lk 17:11–19).

This is one of two cases reported in the Gospels of the healing
of leprosy. Leprosy was a particularly horrible disease, and the leper
frequently was ostracized by his townspeople. Probably the term
"leprosy" was used as a general category for serious skin irritations
caused by the various infectious diseases prevalent in that area. Effective medical treatment was unknown as there were no antibiotics.

This class of diseases must have appeared particularly serious. Suddenly a person's face and other visible areas would be covered with ugly painful sores. Sometimes, just as suddenly, when the illness had run its course and the body's healing forces had defeated the infection, the person would improve and soon the blemishes would be gone. At other times, the body's natural resources were insufficient to overwhelm the infection and the person was left at least scarred and perhaps with a long term infection with recurring sores and swelling.

This was a perfect situation for reinforcing the accepted belief that the illness was a result of sin. It had occurred for no obvious reason and there was no injury or wound. Rather the sores appeared "spontaneously." Might not God, who knew a person's sins, work in this way? And what a perfect way to make the sin known, by writing it all over the person's face. The clearing up of the condition would then mean that the person's repentance had been accepted by God. But the person with the chronic infection had permanently fallen from God's favor.

Again we should not be harsh with a society that tried to understand the cause of the condition and had no other method of understanding than a theological one. To see these diseases as caused by sin gave people some sense of control over them. Don't forget how frightening these illnesses must have been, for they could sometimes have a fatal outcome. This "scapegoating" of people with serious skin conditions was a belief system in itself—i.e., one could hope that God who had caused the illness would relent and bring healing. They knew that God had the power to do so. But they also pictured God as a harsh and strict judge who would publicly embarrass those sinful souls brazen enough to break the rules. This image of God was contradicted by all of Jesus' experiences of a God who longed for all people to enter the Kingdom.

Thus these afflicted people were unwelcome in their society. As unclean sinners, they could "infect" their fellows with their uncleanness. God *expected* people to stay away from these persons so obviously marked as sinners. Notice that these ten "lepers" had formed a community of their own according to different rules. The setting is a border town between Samaria and Galilee. Both Samaritans and Jews were clearly welcomed in the group—being outcasts made them more open to breaking ritual taboos. But there is a tragic element here also. People susceptible to these infections were forced together, which made them even more likely to suffer from chronic infection. Jesus had obviously become a well-known healer by this time. When the ten lepers heard of his arrival they went as a group to plead with him for healing. In response Jesus sent them to the priests, who would declare them clean. They left him without yet being healed. Perhaps some of them were skeptical, not believing he had healed them; perhaps for some, to go to the priests was itself a great demonstration of faith, for they would obviously be seen as unclean if healing had not already taken place.

While traveling they were healed and the Samaritan left the prescribed task to the others. He would not have been welcomed by the priests anyway, for he was unclean by his very heritage. Praising God at the top of his voice he threw himself at Jesus' feet. So grateful was he that he had been healed that he ran back to the source of the healing.

Jesus' first response shows his surprise and annoyance. His own people did not return, but rather continued on to bring themselves back into society. The Samaritan, who still wasn't welcome in Jewish society, returned rejoicing that he was again welcome in God's society. This is an especially poignant scene if we assume that he was the lone Samaritan, for he had become again an outcast to his friends who had returned to their own Samaritan-hating society. He was alone and Jesus was the only one with whom he could celebrate—as he headed back to Samaria to *his* people. Though Jesus wanted the lepers to be restored to society, he seemed upset that the more important "society with God" had taken second place. His frustration perhaps was that the healing had been the end in itself, and the more important coming of the Kingdom where Samaritan and Jew found fellowship still had not occurred.

The Woman with a Hemorrhage

We will now examine the healing of a woman whose illness made her continually unclean and rejected by society.

Now there was a woman suffering from a hemorrhage for twelve years, whom no one had been able to cure. She came up behind him and touched the fringe of his cloak; and the hemorrhage stopped at that instant. Jesus said, "Who touched me?" When they all denied that they had, Peter and his companions said, "Master, it is the crowds around you, pushing." But Jesus said, "Somebody touched me. I felt that power had gone out from me." Seeing herself discovered, the woman came forward trembling, and, falling at his feet, explained in front of all the people why she had touched him and how she had been cured at that very moment. "My daughter," he said, "your faith has restored you to health; go in peace" (Lk 8:43–48).

This disease was viewed by Jews with horror and it rendered the sufferer unclean. The law dealt with it specifically:

If a woman has a discharge of blood for many days, not at the time of her impurity, or if she has a discharge beyond the time of her impurity, all of the days of discharge she shall continue in uncleanness, as in the days of her impurity she shall be unclean. Every bed on which she lies, all the days of her discharge, shall be to her as the bed of her impurity; and everything on which she sits shall be unclean, as in the uncleanness of her impurity. And whoever touches these things shall be unclean, and shall wash his clothes, and bathe himself in water, and be unclean until the evening (Lv 15:25–27).

Here an obvious fear of women's menstrual cycle is evident. A woman with discharge was a walking "infection," unfit for human society. The woman in the story had been in this condition for twelve years. She had been continuously unclean for all this time, unable to participate in communal worship, a virtual outcast. She had by then exhausted all known remedies to no avail. The talmud prescribed eleven cures ranging from tonics and astringents to the superstitious practice of carrying about a barley corn that had been found in the dung of a white she-ass. As the woman walked through the crowds all were unknowingly being made unclean by her when she brushed against them. One wonders why she was not recognized by her townspeople. Perhaps she had traveled to another town where no one would know her so that she could unobtrusively seek healing.

The woman's plan was apparently well thought out and daring. Unclean as she was, she must secretly touch Jesus for healing. She couldn't do what those with other infirmities could do because the social taboo was too great. Though a blind man might say, "Lord, grant me my sight," she could not ask "Lord, would you stop this bleeding?" By sneaking up in the midst of the crowd and touching his cloak, her healing would occur with no one the wiser. She hadn't planned on Jesus "catching her in the act."

Jesus was clearly attuned to the healing power moving through him. His question "Who touched me?" was misunderstood by Peter who himself was being jostled by the crowd. Jesus meant something more by "touch," for a "meeting" had happened. From his side, he had felt power go from him. But he had felt also a "touch," a communication from another person, and he needed to acknowledge it.

The poor woman who had just been healed came forward trembling and "threw herself at his feet and *in front of all the people* confessed." There were not many worse confessions she could have made. The crowds probably grumbled, and many were disgusted by her illness and angered at her audacity. The special "disgrace" of her illness is shown by the fact that, unlike the other healings, this one was not accompanied by expressions of awe, joy and astonishment. This woman was panic-stricken right at the moment of the cure. Jesus, not surprisingly, was not disgusted by her illness but rather restored her to the community, saying in effect: "You are a person of great faith and courage and this has saved you." Had he shown displeasure or disgust the crowds might even have turned on her and harmed her. In Matthew's version (9:20–22), the healing occurred at this point *after* the woman had made herself known. If this were the case she was in even more danger, and her desperation and her faith in coming forward are particularly evident.

This story dramatically demonstrates something of the relationship between Jesus and the persons healed. Not only did power pass between healer and healed, but the faith of the sick person established an intimate connection with Jesus at a deep level of awareness.

At this level—where people were open to the Kingdom—faith was the language of communication. Whenever Jesus experienced the deep faith of another person, the Kingdom seemed to be shared by the two of them. Jesus' experience of the Kingdom was so profound that another's entrance not only could not escape his notice but required that he *recognize* the other. Probably he wanted to see the other to whom power had gone in this situation for he had experienced a jolt and knew that as evidence of the Kingdom.

Healing the Dead

To explore this most difficult and problematic area of the healings done by Jesus, we will now imaginatively enter into Jairus' mind as he begs Jesus to come heal his dying twelve year old daughter (Lk 8:40–56). Recall that Jairus had thrown himself at Jesus' feet, begging him to come and save his daughter. On the way to Jairus' house, in the midst of the crowd, Jesus encountered the woman with a hemorrhage. After that healing, Jesus was again ready to go to Jairus' house.

"You'll come Master? Praise God, let us hurry, for Miriam is very ill."
These crowds! Give us room! Get out of the way! Don't you understand? My daughter is dying! Jesus is going to heal her.

Get out of the way! I must be quiet, not upset him. He has been known to get angry at synagogue officials. God! She is so sick! Hurry, hurry!

What is he stopping for?

"Who touched me?" he asks.

Everybody, everybody, come on! "Somebody *touched* me. I felt that power had gone out from me."

Not the *power!* That is for Miriam! Come! Come! Ach, Veronica! She touched him! No! She's been excluded from worship since before Miriam was born. Don't bother with her. It will make you unclean—what? No matter—just come and save Miriam!

"My daughter, your faith has restored you to health; go in peace."

My daughter is dying! No, here is Thaddeus! I can read his face.

"Your daughter has died," he says gently. "Do not trouble the master any further."

I am going to faint! Aiee! I must faint.

Jesus' arm holds me up.

"Jairus, do not be afraid. Only have faith and she will be saved."

I must be mad! I'm following him! Strange thoughts assail me as we walk. Veronica has been healed—"my daughter." Jesus' daughter lives but mine is dead. Have faith, he says. I do, I must! She is going to live! Veronica has been healed. Her faith saved her! Twelve years I have shunned her. My daughter . . . Miriam . . . They must be wrong. She isn't dead.

Everyone is wailing. Martha, my dear wife, beats her breast. This is tearing her heart out. Our only child!

Have faith! Have faith! Faith, faith, faith . . .

Jesus speaks harshly: "Stop crying; she is not dead, but asleep."

They are laughing at him! No, silence! Have faith. You must have faith.

"Get out of here, all of you!"

Jesus is walking to her bed. He takes her hand.

"Child, get up," he says each word slowly, emphatically.

"My God! Praise my God! Miriam! Oh Martha! She is
alive! My God! Miriam, my dearest one! My God! Oh my God!"

Resurrection from the dead is no doubt the most problematic
possibility of the Kingdom. It is something the thought of which
leaves people shaking their heads. Mental, spiritual and physical
healing are at least comprehensible—to some people. Everyone is
confounded by the notion of resurrection. It defies our experience.
Even if true, it is so rare in human history as to be perhaps meaningless even if magnificent. What difference do these three raisings from
the dead by Jesus two thousand years ago make for us? If no one is
raised before or since those times, what can such raisings mean?

We need not be ashamed if we have difficulty confronting or believing in these resurrections. Indeed, there may be something amiss
in those people who have no difficulty accepting what is recorded in
these three accounts. For it is astounding, awesome, terrifying, hum-
bling, if such events can occur.

The resurrections of Jairus' daughter, Lazarus (Jn 11:1–44) and
the widow of Naim's son (Lk 7:11–17) are extremely important reports. How we understand them, to a great degree, determines how
we understand the Kingdom. For we are here asking a question about
the limits of the Kingdom. Does the Kingdom's power reach only so
far as death and then cease? Either answer to this question is possible
certainly. But if we answer affirmatively, if the Kingdom's power is
limited by death, then it too falls short. God too has been defeated
by the power of death. Now these resurrections are not *necessary* to
prove the power of the Kingdom, but if they did in fact occur, they
are evidence of the far-reaching influence of the Kingdom.

As we have seen, Jesus' vision of the Kingdom was that it is at
the center of the individual and at the center of life. It is the pearl of
great price. Once discovered, a person will sell everything to have it.
It is a place to which everyone is welcome—Pharisee and outcast,
woman and man, Gentile and Jew, clean and unclean.

Does God, does that center which is the Kingdom, desert people at their death? Or is the center also related to death? Does death have a different meaning at that center? If yes, could Jesus who had so powerfully experienced the Kingdom also have found a different relation to death than those who had not experienced the Kingdom? We have suggested that Jesus understood the message of the Kingdom to be that it wants to come into daily life. In other words, Jesus discovered a Kingdom that *already* exists, and he sought to connect earthly life to it, to open people to the awareness and experience of it.

The Kingdom is not a material entity. It has no weight or smell. It is rather a spiritual awareness, an encompassing experience that manifests itself, according to Jesus, by bringing healing to those who need it (Mt 11:2–5), and apparently it is found right at the center, at the heart of the mystery of life and death.

This is the immensity of Jesus' vision. And this is the immensity of the reality of the Kingdom. Given "the faith that can move mountains," even death fits into the experience of the Kingdom. Perhaps God doesn't dichotomize life and death but rather sees them as complementary expressions of a profound mystery. Forces of destructiveness, which Jesus saw so clearly, would rather have us limit ourselves by not seeing that the Kingdom is at our center, by seeing death as the end rather than as part of the mystery.

To see death as part of the mystery is not to suggest that it should be experienced as painless or non-problematic. Death is usually painful and difficult and we would be lying if we denied this. We will now look at the other two accounts of resurrections by Jesus. As you read, notice how clearly the writers portray Jesus' own feelings, particularly in the Lazarus story.

> Now soon afterward he went to a town called Naim, accompanied by his disciples and a great number of people. When he was near the gate of the town it happened that a dead man was being carried out for burial, the only son of his mother, and she was a widow. And a considerable number of the townspeople

were with her. When the Lord saw her he felt sorry for her. "Do not cry," he said. Then he went up and put his hand on the bier and the bearers stood still, and he said, "Young man, I tell you to get up." And the dead man sat up and began to talk, and Jesus gave him to his mother. Everyone was filled with awe and praised God saying, "A great prophet has appeared among us; God has visited his people." And this opinion of him spread throughout Judea and all over the countryside (Lk 7:11–17).

There was a man named Lazarus who lived in the village of Bethany with the two sisters, Mary and Martha, and he was ill. It was the same Mary, the sister of the sick man Lazarus, who anointed the Lord with ointment and wiped his feet with her hair. The sisters sent this message to Jesus, "Lord, the man you love is ill." On receiving the message, Jesus said, "The sickness will end not in death but in God's glory, and through it the Son of God will be glorified."

Jesus loved Martha and her sister and Lazarus, yet when he heard that Lazarus was ill he stayed where he was for two more days before saying to the disciples, "Let us go to Judea." The disciples said, "Rabbi, it is not long since the Jews wanted to stone you: are you going back again?" Jesus replied:

"Are there not twelve hours in the day?
A man can walk in the daytime without stumbling
because he has the light of this world to see by:
but if he walks at night he stumbles,
because there is no light to guide him."

He said that and then added, "Our friend Lazarus is resting. I am going to wake him." The disciples said to him, "Lord, if he is able to rest he is sure to get better." The phrase Jesus used referred to the death of Lazarus, but they thought that by "rest" he meant "sleep," so Jesus put it plainly, "Lazarus is dead; and for your sake I am glad I was not there because now you will believe. But let us go to him." Then Thomas—known as the Twin—said to the other disciples, "Let us go too, and die with him."

On arriving, Jesus found that Lazarus had been in the tomb for four days already. Bethany is only about two miles from Jerusalem, and many Jews had come to Martha and Mary to sympathize with them over their brother. When Martha heard that Jesus had come she went to meet him. Mary remained sitting in the house. Martha said to Jesus, "If you had been here, my brother would not have died, but I know that, even now, whatever you ask of God, he will grant you." "Your brother," said Jesus to her, "will rise again." Martha said, "I know he will rise again at the resurrection on the last day." Jesus said:

"I am the resurrection and the life.

If anyone believes in me, even though he dies he will live.

And whoever lives and believes in me

will never die.

Do you believe this?"

"Yes, Lord," she said, "I believe that you are the Christ, the Son of God, the one who was to come into this world."

When she had said this, she went and called her sister Mary, saying in a low voice, "The Master is here and wants to see you." Hearing this, Mary got up quickly and went to him. Jesus had not yet come into the village; he was still at the place where Martha had met him. When the Jews who were in the house sympathizing with Mary saw her get up so quickly and go out, they followed her, thinking that she was going to the tomb to weep there.

Mary went to Jesus, and as soon as she saw him she threw herself at his feet, saying, "Lord, if you had been here, my brother would not have died." At the sight of her tears, and those of the Jews who followed her, Jesus said in great distress, with a sigh that came straight from the heart, "Where have you put him?" They said, "Lord, come and see." Jesus wept; and the Jews said, "See how much he loved him!" But there were some who remarked, "He opened the eyes of the blind man; could he not have prevented this man's death?" Still sighing, Jesus reached the tomb; it was a cave with a stone to close the opening. Jesus said, "Take the stone away." Martha said to him, "Lord, by now he will smell; this is the fourth day." Jesus replied,

"Have I not told you that if you believe you will see the glory of God?" So they took away the stone. Then Jesus lifted up his eyes and said:

"Father, I thank you for hearing my prayer.
I knew indeed that you always hear me,
but I speak
for the sake of all these who stand around me,
so that they may believe it was you who sent me."

When he had said this, he cried in a loud voice, "Lazarus, here! Come out!" The dead man came out, his feet and hands bound with bands of stuff and a cloth around his face. Jesus said to them, "Unbind him; let him go free" (Jn 11:1–44).

Jesus allowed the feelings that were at the very center of himself to come forth in these resurrections. He let his full humanity be involved when he encountered the deaths of these people. He must have been deeply moved when Jairus threw himself on the ground before him. This act by Jairus so evoked Jesus' compassion that he agreed to come and help Jairus in his extreme need. Or again what more moving scene can be imagined than a widow (still in her clothes of mourning perhaps) beating her breast and wailing at heaven in her overwhelming misery at the loss of her son? Jesus who felt so deeply must have been profoundly affected by her and his response came out of his compassion for her. Then, finally, his own friend had died, and his own friends were mourning, blaming him for not coming sooner. Their grief was practically thrown at him when he arrived and he responded with a "sigh that came straight from the heart," and then he wept. In this last situation, his compassion mingled with his own grief and loss.

There is a compelling similarity in these stories. Jesus acts with compassion in response to each death. This is just what he has done for those who were afflicted physically, mentally, or spiritually. His reaction to death was a "Kingdom response"; it was the desire to manifest the Kingdom that brought forth these healings of death. Herein lies the great mystery of these resurrections. From the center of himself came his compassion, and it is at that very center that he had discovered the Kingdom. His full humanity seems to have been the channel of these great acts. Anything less than compassion—than truly suffering with the sufferers—could not have brought the Kingdom experience to these deaths. It is as though the ability to be fully human, to be truly compassionate to others, shows one the heart of God out of which comes the mystery of life and love.

If this is a correct understanding, then death is not beyond the power of the Kingdom. But that death for the one who dies is not thereby necessarily a horrible experience; it does not necessarily send one to a horrible "place." Perhaps those who died had even experienced the Kingdom while they were dead and would be able to share their experience with their loved ones on their return. Jesus' compassion, however, was for those who were left behind, who did not experience the Kingdom but rather were deeply grieved by the loss of their loved ones. Jesus, who had experienced the Kingdom so intimately, who knew that it encompassed life and death, who saw that death was necessary for new life, sought to use these particular deaths to show people—in a most dramatic and shocking way—the existence and the power of the Kingdom. Though their loved ones had been restored to them, imagine the challenge presented to them whenever they recalled that this beloved person who stood before them had once been dead.

I have sought in this section to wonder about what the healing of death might mean. Certainly, I don't claim to have proven that these resurrections occurred but rather to show that they fit into the logic of the Kingdom. Each of us is left, as were the listeners of the story of the prodigal. Each is asked the same questions: "Did these three people come back from the dead? Does the Kingdom have power even over death?"

6.

Prayer

From the moment we meet the adult Jesus at the beginning of the Gospels to the very end of his life at Gethsemane and Golgotha, we encounter a man whose life was filled with prayer. After his profound experience of baptism, he immediately went to the desert to pray. After long days among the people he withdrew to pray. When he healed persons, he prayed. As he prepared to face torture, he prayed. Even as he died he continued to pray.

In a culture so devoted to things spiritual, it is of course no surprise to find Jesus praying. But the Gospels tell us that certain aspects of Jesus' prayer were different than the generally accepted practices.

PRAYER IN SOLITUDE

Most noticeable to the person who combs the Gospels seeking examples of Jesus' prayer is that so few explicit prayers are reported. What is usually found instead are statements like: "He went off by himself to pray," and "He awoke early and went off to the hills to pray." It seems obvious that Jesus regularly needed time alone to consider what was happening, to be restored, and to be with God. From the beginning of his public life (and probably before), Jesus found

111

himself in an intimate and deepening relationship with God. His private relationship with God developed when he was by himself, for when he was with others, their pleas and concerns captured his attention. Quite likely, his times of lonely prayer prevented what modern health professionals call "the burnout syndrome"; in the silence he was restored, refreshed and reconnected with God.

Remember the goal that ruled Jesus' behavior: to bring people an awareness that the Kingdom of heaven was happening in their very midst. In attempting to reach this goal Jesus undoubtedly became discouraged by the stubbornness of the religious leaders, the immensity of suffering around him, and the inability of people to hold on to the awareness of the Kingdom. He must have felt a lulling pull to re-enter the social trance. Only by returning frequently to the source of the Kingdom could he be renewed and sustain himself against this collective attitude.

He tried to emphasize this to his listeners:

> When you pray go to your private room and when you have shut the door, pray to your Father who is in that secret place, and your Father who sees all that is done in secret will reward you (Mt 6:6).

Contrary to the scribes and Pharisees, who believed they had *already* found and understood God and were showing others by their public praying, fasting, teaching and tithing how to find God, Jesus here suggested that God was to be found in the lonely place within oneself, that place which no one knew, and not in actions paraded in front of people to prove one's holiness. That quiet place, like the mustard seed buried under the ground, was where the spark of the Kingdom ignited, where God met the person directly and in secret. It was not critical that others knew about this meeting; Jesus seemed to consider it a positive danger for persons to try to prove their own goodness by showing that they prayed well, because they would be filled with pride. Being with God in that secret place where one's heart was known would in itself prevent the person from being full of pride, Jesus implies, because there one's sins and hidden secrets lurked. But God, knowing this, would not punish the person for the sin, but instead reward the person who had come to the secret place to pray.

Jesus' remarks on fasting stress the same point:

> When you fast do not put on a gloomy look as the hypocrites do; they pull long faces to let men know they are fasting. I tell you solemnly, they have had their reward. But when you fast, put oil on your head and wash your face, so that no one will know you are fasting except your Father who sees all that is done in secret; and your Father who sees all that is done in secret will reward you (Mt 6:16–18).

Again the private prayerful act reaped its own reward. "Gloomy looks" were meant to impress others, not to honor God. By fasting in private, one bet all on God; having sacrificed the recognition of others, only what was found in the inner secret place mattered. And God, who saw *why* one was fasting in this way, gave the reward. Perhaps when he was asked by the scribes and Pharisees (Lk 5:33) why *his* disciples didn't fast when the disciples of John the Baptist did, he could have answered "Fools! They *do* fast and still are joyous. They aren't trying to impress you. They are seeking God."

Jesus in his teachings sought to bring others into the relationship with God that was the Kingdom. No outward show of piety could accomplish this, but only quiet and lonely prayer at the heart of oneself. Jesus, whose every move was watched by crowds of people, could himself only maintain this relationship by getting away to a private place where he could be with God and experience the richness and power of the Kingdom.

THREE STORIES ABOUT PRAYER

In the following three well-known stories Jesus brilliantly expressed his understanding of prayer and its relationship to the Kingdom.

The Call at Midnight

> Suppose one of you has a friend and goes to him in the middle of the night to say, "My friend, lend me three loaves, because a friend of mine on his travels has just arrived at my house and I have nothing to offer him"; and the man answers from inside the house, "Do not bother me. The door is bolted now, and my children and I are in bed; I cannot get up to give it to you." I tell you, if the man does not get up and give it him for friendship's sake, persistence will be enough to make him get up and give his friend all he wants (Lk 11:5–8).

In Mideastern society, hospitality to guests was (and still is) of primary importance. To mistreat a guest was to bring shame on oneself, and in Palestine shame was rigorously avoided. In this story, the host went to a neighbor to ask for bread to help feed his guest. In a Palestinian village, a guest was the responsibility of the whole community, not just the host. Jesus' listeners would have known that the man inside would typically have opened the door to his neighbor automatically; the excuses of sleeping children and a locked door would have been flimsy and unthinkable to a Palestinian audience.

In verse 8, the word translated above as "persistence" is *anaideia*. Commentators argue for two translations of this Greek word in this passage. The word may be translated as "persistence" and it then refers to the caller. Jesus would then be inviting his listeners to identify with this caller. In Palestinian culture, the caller is acting properly by seeking food from fellow villagers. The Palestinian listeners of this story would fully expect the sleeper to respond immediately and would have been surprised at even the suggestion of refusal. The caller's request for bread is also significant in that bread is a staple at every meal, the "knife and spoon" used for dipping into the common eating bowls. He is asking the sleeper for the most basic and rudimentary item and can expect his persistence to pay off because of the strength of his request. The whole community is behind him and would be shamed if the guest were treated poorly. Even this tired fellow would automatically accede to the caller's requests. Any other response would be unthinkable to the original listeners.

The second translation of *anaideia* is more literal. Kenneth Bailey in his book *Poet and Peasant* argues eloquently that the Greek word is better translated as "shamelessness" and that persistence became the favored term because it was unthinkable for the Christian community to consider God and shamelessness in the same breath. In a shame culture, as we have seen, avoidance of shame is the utmost priority. If we substitute shamelessness for persistence verse 8 reads: "I tell you, if the man does not get up and give it him for friendship's sake, shamelessness will be enough to make him get up and give his friend all he wants." Shamelessness would then refer to the man in bed, not the caller outside. His sense of shame before his village would prevent him from ignoring the request; refusal to get up would be reported to the whole village by the host and everyone would be angry at this insult to the guest because he was *their* guest also. The desire to be without shame would push the sleeper to respond even if friendship did not. It was virtually unthinkable to these Palestinian listeners that he would deny the request.

What does this story have to say about prayer? Part of the answer is found in the passage directly following this story (Lk 11:9–13) which we will consider later in the chapter. Here remember the principle *kal va homer*. If you go to your neighbor with everything against you—it is late, the door is locked, everyone is asleep—even then will this man who has a sense of integrity give you not only the bread but *all* you ask for. How much more then will God who is true and good answer your request for what is needed?

Jesus seemed to be telling them that it is just as unthinkable that God will not answer one's prayers. Furthermore, persistence (taking the first translation) in prayer affirms and strengthens the one who prays. Jesus apparently wanted his hearers to understand that they were justified in being persistent in prayer, that what they prayed for was as much their right as the request of the caller for bread for his guest.

Notice finally that Jesus was talking about seeking what was needed to show hospitality to another. Thus he was asking his listeners to bring their concern *for others* to God in this way and to trust that God would answer.

The Persistent Widow

> Then he told them a parable about the need to pray continually and never lose heart. "There was a judge in a certain town," he said, "who had neither fear of God nor respect for man. In the same town there was a widow who kept on coming to him and saying, 'I want justice from you against my enemy!' For a long time he refused, but at last he said to himself, 'Maybe I have neither fear of God nor respect for man, but since she keeps pestering me I must give this widow her just rights, or she will persist in coming and worry me to death.' "
>
> And the Lord said, "You notice what the unjust judge has to say? Now will not God see justice done to his chosen who cry to him day and night even when he delays to help them? I promise you, he will see justice done to them, and done speedily. But when the Son of Man comes, will he find any faith on earth?" (Lk 18:1–8).

Jesus would not tell a parable "about the need to pray continually and never lose heart" if there were not present danger that some of his followers would in fact lose heart. The way to the Kingdom was extremely difficult, as Jesus saw, and one must take precautions to accomplish it.

It is well known that many judges in Jerusalem were corrupt

and could be financially persuaded to turn a case toward one of the parties. One wonders if in this instance the widow's antagonist had already paid off the judge. In any case, this particular judge had no shame before God or man. While a major motivating factor for people in a shame culture is often the desire to save face, the judge had no interest at all in this. He didn't really care what others or even God thought of him. To these Palestinian listeners who were so aware of shame and the need to avoid being shamed, this judge would have been despicable.

The widow *continually* (*eis telos* in the Greek) pleaded with this unscrupulous judge for justice. Ordinarily in the Mideast a woman did not go to court herself; rather a man from her extended family went to represent her case. Mideastern listeners would assume since she had gone herself that she had no man in her family to do this for her and was thus totally alone. To be a widow alone put her at the mercy of the judge. It is hard to imagine a better figure to represent one who might lose faith. And yet this widow did just the opposite and finally wore out the unjust judge with her insistent begging. If such a man could act thus toward the persistent widow, how much more would God help those "who cry to him day and night?"

If Jesus' listeners lost heart, there would be no one on earth to help bring about the Kingdom. Jesus knew personally the spiritual and social forces of destructiveness that worked against him and his little band of followers. The tension would crush them, the Kingdom would not come into being, unless they prayed continually. If they could see even this helpless widow persevere and get justice done, they might be able to believe that against the impossible odds God would hear their prayers and lead them into the Kingdom.

The second paragraph of this parable is somewhat disturbing. Why would God *delay* to help? What is this reference to the Son of Man? One is reminded of the need to persist knocking in the preceding parable of the caller at midnight. Does this suggest that God "tests" followers to see how strong and persistent their faith is? Perhaps the second paragraph of the present parable is an addition by the early Church which was suffering persecution. Perhaps the paragraph was added as an encouragement to the persons in the Christian community who were losing heart. The early Church believed that Christ ("the Son of Man") would soon return to set up his Kingdom. If none of the faithful persevered there would be no Kingdom to set up. Or perhaps this is a statement Jesus himself made to his frightened followers so that they might see that though God's actions weren't presently evident, even those with least to be hopeful for, like the widow in our story, had reason to persist. In either case, the idea of God delaying to help is a distressing one. Those struggling with persecution in the early Christian era and in our own time often wrestle with this sense that God is absent. Perhaps Jesus was suggesting that persistent prayer finally broke through this feeling of absence and brought the bereft sufferer into the Kingdom of God's presence.

The Pharisee and the Publican

> He spoke the following parable to some people who prided themselves on being virtuous and despised everyone else, "Two men went up to the temple to pray, one a Pharisee, the other a tax collector. The Pharisee stood by himself there and said this prayer, 'I thank you, God, that I am not grasping, unjust, adulterous like the rest of mankind, and particularly that I am not like this tax collector here. I fast twice a week; I pay tithes on all I get.' The tax collector stood some distance away, not daring even to raise his eyes to heaven; but he beat his breast and said, 'God, be merciful to me, a sinner.' This man, I tell you, went home again at rights with God; the other did not. For everyone who exalts himself will be humbled, but the man who humbles himself will be exalted" (Lk 18:9–14).

This beautiful story contains the essence of Jesus' attitude toward prayer. The two men were standing in the temple praying. It is likely that they were at the daily atonement service where a lamb was sacrificed for the sins of the people. Thus other people were nearby who were themselves praying for forgiveness. The Pharisee, rather than seeking forgiveness, boasted of his goodness. His "prayer" likely was said aloud, for that was the Hebrew custom. Thus others present heard his boastfulness and his disdain for them, "the rest of mankind," and for the tax collector, that turncoat who defiled himself among pagans while stealing from his own people. Remember that the tax collector was a rejected outcast. The Pharisee supported that rejecting attitude with his words and thus effected a double separation: himself from all of the people and all of them from the tax collector.

In reality the tax collector was a broken man out of fellowship with his people, praying fervently to God that he might be taken back into his people's fellowship at this atonement service. He beat his breast while praying, which is something Mideastern men do only when they are intensely angry or in extreme anguish. His prayer, unlike the Pharisee's, put him right with God because he prayed honestly from the heart. The Pharisee really didn't pray at all, but used the sacrificial service to show others how he not only kept the law but even bettered it. This Pharisee epitomizes the attitude that Jesus criticized in Matthew 6:5. There could be no spiritual reward for those who acted in this way because they separated themselves both from other people and from God.

THE DISCIPLES AND PRAYER

Most of the recorded cases of Jesus at prayer have him totally by himself (e.g., Mt 14:23; Mk 1:35; 1:47; Lk 6:12). This we have suggested was because he needed quiet to be restored in his relationship with God. There are accounts, however, in which Jesus prays alone with his disciples. In Luke 9:18 Jesus was praying alone *in the presence of* his disciples. This is a very interesting image. Imagine Jesus sitting quietly, eyes closed, breathing peacefully while his disciples sat to one side watching, wondering what was going on within him but perhaps aware that he was communing with God. This image suggests that Jesus could find a place of quietness with his disciples, that sometimes it wasn't necessary for him to get away totally by himself. Something of the intimacy of his relationship with them speaks through this image. Jesus trusted them enough to enter into a prayerful meditative state in front of them, and they who usually asked him so many questions respected his time of silence.

There is the added possibility that Jesus was "modeling" for them his meditative form of prayer through which he obtained so many of his insights. He seemed to have judged them open enough to enter into prayer "in the secret place" and perhaps was showing them how he did it. At any rate, he emerged from this prayer with the question: "Who do the crowds say I am?"

> And they answered, "John the Baptist; others Elijah, and others say one of the ancient prophets come back to life." "But you," he said, "who do you say I am?" It was Peter who spoke up. "The Christ of God," he said. But he gave them strict orders not to tell anyone anything about this (Lk 9:19–21).

The dialogue portrays the different perceptions that the disciples and the crowds had of Jesus. However, we also see throughout the Gospels times when Jesus was totally frustrated with the disciples for not understanding. Jesus himself seemed better able to hold onto the awareness of the Kingdom even in difficult situations while his followers tended to lose sight of it under duress. This is one reason Jesus saw prayer as so terribly important. The pull of social expectations and structures worked against the Kingdom and made it much more difficult to perceive. Finding God in the secret place encouraged one and sank one's roots into the Kingdom. That the Kingdom and the prevailing social values were at odds is evident in the statement about being his follower.

> Then to all he said, "If anyone wants to be a follower of mine, let him renounce himself and take up his cross every day and follow me. For anyone who wants to save his life will lose it; but

anyone who loses his life for my sake, that man will save it. What gain, then, is it for a man to have won the whole world and to have lost or ruined his very self?" (Lk 9:23–26).

The Kingdom and social values worked against one another. One could not serve two masters but instead had to choose between them. Prayer, Jesus saw, was a way to experience the Kingdom. There one could determine more readily the value of choosing the Kingdom for one would be in the loving, forgiving presence of God.

The Inner Circle. Jesus did not see all the disciples as equally open to the depths of his message about the Kingdom. He reportedly took Peter, James and John up a mountain to the place of his transfiguration but left the others behind. Perhaps he perceived these three disciples as most open to experiencing the Kingdom. The four of them entered a collective altered or visionary state of awareness, one perhaps to which the other disciples could not yet obtain. In fact, the other disciples might have been a deterrent to the occurrence of the visionary experience. At any rate, the three disciples saw Jesus in the presence of two beings they recognized as Moses and Elijah. Boisterous Peter proposed that three tents be made to mark the event. Just then a cloud came and covered them with shadow.

> When they went into the cloud the disciples were afraid. And a voice came from the cloud saying, "This is my Son, the Chosen One. Listen to him." And after the voice had spoken, Jesus was found alone. The disciples kept silence and, at that time, told no one what they had seen (Lk 9:34–36).

Their different reaction to the event tells us something about both Jesus and his disciples. The cloud from which the voice spoke frightened the disciples out of their wits. Peter had been effusive about the vision until the voice spoke. God, who was experienced by Jesus as a loving parent, frightened them. To them God was primarily the powerful, fearful Unknown. Until they understood Jesus' message God could only be experienced thus. No wonder they heeded Jesus' request that they keep quiet. They probably did not want to think too much about the experience themselves. Jesus, on the other hand, seemed more adept at moving from ordinary to visionary reality and back. He apparently had a deeper and more trusting relationship with God that developed out of his own many encounters with the forgiving One in the secret place. The ending of the account is quite remarkable in its straightforward simplicity. The others were gone and Jesus was alone with his disciples. The visionary state had passed, leaving his disciples upset and shaken while Jesus remained composed, continuing his policy of secrecy and ready to descend the mountain to again meet the people.

The Outer Circle. Immediately, as we have seen, Jesus met the crowds and his other disciples who had failed to heal the epileptic demoniac. When Jesus had accomplished this, his disciples asked him why they had been unable to cast out the demon. According to Mark's account, Jesus answered "This is the kind that can only be driven out by prayer" (9:29). But prayer of such depth was no easy matter, so fearful were people of encountering God. Matthew's account has Jesus say that they were unsuccessful because they had "little faith" (17:20). There is a sort of catch-22 here. To make healing possible one had to have faith. But faith required trust in a loving, forgiving God, and it was difficult to have such trust without seeing evidence of this loving, forgiving God, for example, in healing. Again we see why Jesus taught about the Kingdom in shocking ways, for only by being shocked could people break through this catch-22 situation and perceive the Kingdom.

HOW TO PRAY

The disciples saw something of the connection between Jesus' prayers and his great faith and ability. In Luke's version, the prayer

Jesus taught came in response to the request that they too might learn to pray as he did. He told them to say this when they prayed:

> "Father, may your name be held holy.
> Your kingdom come;
> give us each day our daily bread,
> and forgive us our sins,
> for we ourselves forgive each one who is in debt to us.
> And do not put us to the test" (Lk 11:2–4).

If you read quickly through Luke's account, you probably noticed that certain verses of the popular version of the Lord's Prayer are missing. Matthew's account (6:9–13) more closely approximates our modern prayer. Both prayers ask first of all that God may be recognized and that the Kingdom may come. The first task of prayer was to enter into an awareness of God's presence and to pray for God's purpose to become reality.

God was addressed by Jesus by the altogether startling title Abba, which means daddy. The person who prayed thus was to recognize that the Holy One whose purpose was to bring the Kingdom was like a daddy, intimate, loving, and involved with his children. So often have we heard this prayer that we miss the shocking dissonance of the Most Holy One being presented as Papa. Never before had such a thing been suggested. The prayer tells us as much about Jesus' own relationship with God as it tells us about how to pray, and is one of the most jolting statements in all of his teaching. Jesus then told the disciples to ask this "daddy" to meet their daily needs. God, according to Jesus, did not want to save people from the world so much as to come into it and to be with them there. The next request in the prayer was for forgiveness, which came about only as one entered an awareness of one's forgiveness for others. The disciples were thus instructed to pray for an attitude of forgiveness that itself made God's forgiveness known.

"Do not put us to the test" was a curious statement to make to a daddy. Perhaps it was a humble acknowledgement that one saw the danger of being overcome by such a test and that one's first desire was the Kingdom and not recognition as a hero. There is a deep honesty in this request by Jesus. It admits that life is often problematic. Certainly people go through horrible experiences when it feels as though God is testing them or else is idly standing by while they are being destroyed. Jesus acknowledged the dark events of life here. We might call this the "Job problem" in human life. People can be destroyed in this life and not understand where God is. Further, Jesus may have seen that individuals have to participate in their relationship with God. To ask not to be tested would then be the person's joining with God in dialogue to "work out" together what is best for that person. Implicit in this notion is that a person's prayer can presumably sway God or "change God's mind." Perhaps Jesus believed that God was open to creative suggestions from persons about their lives. Finally, a terrible irony resides in this phrase for Jesus was put to the ultimate test. It is quite likely that *he* knew what it meant to be put to the test. His life was one in which God made numerous requests. To pray that one not be tested is thus a poignant expression of the struggle of Jesus in his own life and his admission that people should take seriously their relationship with God because God may ask the ultimate of them.

Two other phrases appear in Matthew's version, which is placed in the midst of the teachings at the Sermon on the Mount. "Your will be done on earth as in heaven" (6:10) is perhaps an amplification (whether by Jesus or an author in the early Church) on the preceding "Your kingdom come," for the coming of the Kingdom on earth was precisely what Jesus understood as God's will. By praying this, one put oneself "in synch" with the coming of the Kingdom and gave oneself over to God's greater authority. Second, "Save us from the evil one" (6:13) is an acknowledgement that there exists a powerful destructive force that works against the Kingdom. People who would enter the Kingdom had to beware of their formidable foe.

Evil has been a perennial problem through human history. Consciousness has always forced people to see that there is something "not quite right" in the universe. Conversely, that something good and creative resides at life's center has been a perennial vision of humanity. These two perceptions being so, the aching question "whence evil" has echoed through the ages. Almost every society has developed its own elaborate cosmology to explain the existence of evil. It is here a fallen angel, there a twin of the good God, still elsewhere capitalism, death or cancer. Though the explanations differ, the intent is the same. People feel in their bowels the not-rightness of life, the evil influences pervading life. Jesus' own experience and teaching was directed at battling this pervasive evil which perverted societies and destroyed the health and spirit of individuals. The destructiveness of this "non-rightness of the universe" is self-evident. The prayer to be saved from it is a statement that Jesus believes that God can battle this evil and further that God wants to, i.e., this "non-rightness" is not right in God's eyes either. It is in the Kingdom that the love of God is to bring transformation and restore persons and life to their basic "rightness."

In Luke's account the teaching of the Lord's Prayer is followed by the parable of the importunate friend which we examined earlier in this chapter and then Jesus' statement about effective prayer.

> So I say to you: Ask, and it will be given to you; search, and you will find; knock, and the door will be opened to you. For the one who asks always receives; the one who searches always finds; the one who knocks will always have the door opened to him. What father among you would hand his son a stone when he asked for bread? Or hand him a snake instead of a fish? Or hand him a scorpion if he asked for an egg? If you then, who are evil, know how to give your children what is good, how much more will the heavenly Father give the Holy Spirit to those who ask him (Lk 11:9–13).

In this strong directive, Jesus tells his listeners in no uncertain terms the attitude with which to pray. Notice that he speaks in the imperative voice; he is, in effect, *commanding* his listeners to pray in this way. There is something startling in his approach. Perhaps again he wants to startle his hearers, to put the problem directly in their laps. At first sight, the command seems to put them in a difficult position for they seem to be expected to tell God what to do. Their experience probably tells many of them that they don't always get what they ask for or find what they seek. Jesus doesn't seem to be telling his listeners that every earthly wish will be fulfilled; sorrows will still come, difficulties will still have to be faced. But he does guarantee that each prayer will be heard and that God will send the Holy Spirit in response to their seeking. Perhaps Jesus used the imperative voice for the same reason parents often do. A command forces the hearer to listen more carefully. In this case a command helped make his difficult message more clear. On one level, everyone knew that God did not "make everything all right" in their day-to-day lives. This probably made most of them unaware of the ongoing action of God. Jesus seemed to believe that God was always present, eager to establish the Kingdom. People could come to awareness of God's actions by praying, as Jesus taught, with confidence and hope. By expecting the Holy Spirit, their eyes were set toward a different type of action from God. None of this argument, incidentally, precludes the possibility of God acting directly and, for example, healing an illness.

Jesus seems to have been seeking to create an attitude in his listeners. He used several powerful images to dramatize his point. It was unthinkable that they would give a stone to a child who asked for bread. He thus put his listeners into "God's place" for a moment. "If your child asked you for something, how would *you* respond?" Then using again the teaching principle, *kal va homer,* he showed that God would do even more. The phrase "you who are evil" is perhaps problematic. Jesus may have been using this phrase for a double purpose. First, he suggests that an impulse toward goodness exists in his hearers—they wouldn't hand their child a scorpion instead of an egg. The statement thus has a paradoxical effect. "You who are evil" have in you a natural tendency toward good. This does not deny, of course, other tendencies toward evil. Second, God wants even more that we have what we want and need. In fact, Jesus seems to be saying that God will give *more* than is requested; the Holy Spirit is God's response to prayer. In other words, when people pray fervently, they are given the heart of God and invited into the Kingdom. Sometimes this may mean that one's objective request is answered immediately. Sometimes it may rather mean that one acquires a deeper understanding of one's request.

Jesus' central message was the coming of the Kingdom. In his own prayer he seemed to find a deep and abiding experience of that Kingdom. God could in fact be addressed by the shocking term Abba. This indicates that Jesus felt great intimacy for and from God. The great Center of all things could be tender and loving. This was a hard message for Jesus to get through to people who suffered the trials of earthly life. Only by his own actions and behavior could he make believable what he himself experienced about the love of God.

7.

Intimacy

When we think of Jesus, the emotion we perhaps most often associate him with is love. Less frequently do we consider the ramifications of this for Jesus himself. Jesus' thoughts, stories and behavior grew out of his own passionate experience of God and the Kingdom. His desire to incarnate this Kingdom was a powerful factor in his teaching and behavior. His own experience showed him that God was so close to him as to be accurately called "daddy." In his desert experience he experienced a profound and passionate parental love which was so ecstatic that he was utterly and literally brought outside himself and changed forever. In that deep secret place God was so real and so present as to be tangibly felt—more real than anything he had ever known before. Unlike the outer temple sacrifices which were offered to a judging, legalistic Creator, this experience brought people into passionate and intimate relationship with a dear parent.

Such a radical departure from the traditional imagery of God could be understood only on its own terms. Until one met God oneself and sensed God to be a loving forgiving parent, it was virtually impossible to understand Jesus' teachings on love. Ritual was important to Jesus only as it brought one to that place of relationship with God. When ritual became the end in itself, or the proof of righteousness, it ceased to have merit. It then became a prison which blocked one's entrance into the reality where one met God and entered intimate relationship with God.

As we have seen, the notion of intimate relationship with God was a startling one to Jesus' contemporaries. The Pharisees frequently complained that Jesus claimed to know the very heart of God. And their complaints were justified, for he did claim this. The Pharisees who were spiritually imprisoned were threatened by his free intimacy with God. Seeking righteousness through outer acts, they did not like the idea of a Kingdom where one must look beyond one's actions to their source within one's heart.

Jesus' teaching on love really is deeply intimate, perhaps embarrassingly so. He refused to accept society's rules for intimacy. This is evidenced very dramatically in his general command to love one's enemies and in the story of the Samaritan (Lk 10:29–37) that we examined earlier. It was shocking enough that the Samaritan, who usually represented what Jews found most hateful, was the example of love. But even worse, the *rules* of loving were virtually dissolved and the standard societal reference points ignored as Jesus' listeners were thrown into new spiritual territory. Passion was not fulfilled in hatred of enemies and love of friends and family. The passion that came from meeting God in intimacy burst all bounds of logic, propriety and legality, demolished all obstructive rules, and spilled forth its new meaning. People were not justified simply by loving those who had been defined as friends by accident of birth, lineage, race, sex, or fulfillment of predetermined ritual. For that is not love at all, not in its passionate sense!

This God whose Kingdom Jesus proclaimed must have seemed worse than illegitimate and unrighteous to the scribes and Pharisees. Jesus' Abba sounded something of a spendthrift and prostitute, loving beyond rules, boundaries, and propriety, loving shamelessly those who had been defined as unlovable and those who had disregarded important rules. No God of Israel could love Israel's enemies! But such was the passion of the intimate God whose Kingdom Jesus sought.

Thus we can understand Jesus' strange teachings, stories and actions in a deep and personal way. The God he experienced in the desert burst all previous boundaries of understanding. God's loving forgiveness so overwhelmed whatever sin had been committed that the sin could no longer stand. Staying *out* of intimate relationship with God became a statement of extreme pridefulness. In the Kingdom it took more power than one had to overcome God's loving forgiveness and there one experienced in deepest humility the powerful paradox of an intimate Ruler and Creator. So bountiful was the Kingdom that people were paid a full day's wages for just showing up (Mt 20:1–6), and reaped a full harvest for just planting the seed (Mt 13:8), and were overwhelmingly rewarded for investing wisely whatever amount they had been given (Mt 25:14–30). He brought this passionate, overwhelmingly intimate God to all who were ignored and rejected and showed them God's passionate love for them.

JESUS AND WOMEN

Women have a low status in patriarchal societies. Their roles are usually few and well-defined such as childbearing and childrearing and raising food in the garden. Normally, no honors, significant political power or religious posts are open to women in these societies. Such was the situation in Palestinian society in the time of Jesus. Israelite women of legitimate families fulfilled their marital expectations by providing their husbands with sons. Condolences were given to parents when a daughter was born. Further, a daughter had to be supported by her father and brothers until she married. If a marriage could not be readily arranged, this frequently brought financial hardship on her family.

Few social benefits came to women in Palestinian society. As discussed earlier, the woman who trespassed against society's restrictions could be easily divorced—which in that culture meant that she must support herself. This effectively made her an outcast, for few occupations were open to the divorced woman beyond prostitution, and this profession made her unclean. Non-Jewish women and women from families with blemish were held in even lower esteem by Jewish society. There was a saying that "the heathen has no father"; based on this all heathen women were suspected of prostitution.

Sexuality

Women also bore a specific psychological burden in Palestinian society, though it was generally unrecognized. Women "carried" their society's sexuality. The men in that society seemed to deny their own sexuality, their own sexual responsibility. The prostitute, who carried the society's sexuality, was consistently unclean while the man who used her sexually was unclean for only a brief period of time. Woman then was like a sexual scapegoat; she bore the responsibility of this unacceptable passion, and her only useful function was the procreation of sons. The prostitute was in actuality what each woman was potentially. It was considered disgraceful for a man to look at a married woman or to be alone with a woman. For the same reason, scholars would not talk to women on the street. This then was a case of projected sexuality where men placed their rejected, hated passion onto women and then punished the women for it. Legitimate Israelites did not incorporate their own sexuality as part of their spiritual wholeness. Jesus who was himself a legitimate Jew was subject to the same ritual sanctions and social disapproval for mingling with women of questionable morals or status. But Jesus had had his own passionate intimate experience—with God—and thus he understood and accepted women as his contemporaries could not. Indeed, being passionate himself, it is no wonder that he was drawn to passionate people such as these prostitutes.

The Woman Caught in Adultery. Perhaps the story of the woman caught in adultery best shows the radical difference between Jesus' perceptions of women and those of the religious leaders of his time.

At daybreak he appeared in the temple again; and as all the people came to him, he sat down and began to teach them. The scribes and Pharisees brought a woman along who had been caught committing adultery; and making her stand there in full view of everybody, they said to Jesus, "Master, this woman was caught in the very act of committing adultery and Moses has ordered us in the law to condemn women like this to death by stoning. What have you to say?" They asked him this as a test, looking for something to use against him. But Jesus bent down and started writing on the ground with his finger. As they persisted with their question, he looked up and said, "If there is one of you who has not sinned, let him be the first to throw a stone at her." Then he bent down and wrote on the ground again. When they heard this they went away one by one, beginning with the eldest, until Jesus was left alone with the woman, who remained standing there. He looked up and said, "Woman, where are they? Has no one condemned you?" "No one sir," she replied. "Neither do I condemn you," said Jesus. "Go and don't sin anymore" (Jn 8:2–11).

According to this account, the scribes and Pharisees claim to have caught this woman in the "very act of adultery." Picture how this happened. Did the scribes and Pharisees enter someone's house to catch them? Was it a setup? How did they know that this meeting was going on? To be caught in the very act obviously presupposes that she was not by herself. Where then was the man with whom she had been consorting? Why was he not there also about to be stoned to death? By law, he should also have been stoned (e.g., Dt 22:22). Did stoning the woman suffice to make up for the act of adultery? And if so, why? It was a curious situation that was presented to Jesus. He was being asked his opinion on the woman's fate but nothing about the man with whom she had been intimate. The double standard of the scribes and Pharisees is glaringly visible in this example.

Jesus seized the opportunity to expose the unfair and unequal value system of the scribes, Pharisees and society. They were using the law of Moses to justify their own attitudes. If they were simply interested in upholding the law, they would certainly have brought along the guilty man also. But sexuality is a passion that resists rules and often transgresses them. The woman seems to have been considered the guilty party. Perhaps she had enticed the man into bed. Apparently she had agreed to have sex with him, and this was immoral and against the law.

Jesus refused to let her accusers use their projections destructively. He knew that all of them had their own secret sins which they could not deny. By making sinlessness the determinant to commence stoning, he shocked them into withdrawing their projections from her and put them beside her in judgment. They, however, could quietly absorb the shock of being shown their sins and walk away, although possibly some of their attitudes were transformed by Jesus' challenge.

After all the others had gone, the two of them stood there alone for a few moments. Often Jesus' final statement, "Go and don't sin anymore," is emphasized as the teaching of this story, but this interpretation misses the richness and intimacy of the situation. How grateful the woman must have felt! Just a moment before she had stood at death's door and he had rescued her. How could she possibly thank him? How embarrassed she must have been before this man who knew her sin!

Jesus quickly dealt with this concern by stating that he didn't accuse her for what she had done. Something unspoken may have passed between them. Jesus who so knew overpowering passion that he risked his life for it may have conveyed this passion to her. To tell her to sin no more would then have been a statement between two passionate people. Rather than telling her that God would "get" her if she sinned again, might he not have been showing her passion's higher purpose? Passion told her of God if only she could recognize it. He didn't want her to snuff out her passion ("neither do I condemn you"), but to recognize it as a part of her wholeness, of her value as a person created by God. To sin again would be to think too small, to miss the fact that her passion could guide her to God rather than condemn her to death and disgrace. Jesus had accepted his own passionate nature as that which opened him to God's overpowering and transforming love. Out of this self-understanding came acceptance and understanding of this woman's passion.

The Woman Who Was a Sinner. In the following story, we see Jesus' response to a grand and passionate gesture of love.

> One of the Pharisees invited him to a meal. When he arrived at the Pharisee's house and took his place at table, a woman came in, who had a bad name in the town. She had heard he was dining with the Pharisee and had brought with her an alabaster jar of ointment. She waited behind him at his feet, weeping, and her tears fell on his feet, and she wiped them away with her hair; then she covered his feet with kisses and anointed them with the ointment.
>
> When the Pharisee who had invited him saw this, he said to himself, "If this man were a prophet, he would know who this woman is that is touching him and what a bad name she has." Then Jesus took him up and said, "Simon, I have something to say to you." "Speak Master," was the reply. "There was once a creditor who had two men in his debt; one owed him five hundred denarii, the other fifty. They were unable to pay, so he pardoned them both. Which of them will love him more?" "The one who was pardoned more, I suppose," answered Simon. Jesus said. "You are right."
>
> Then he turned to the woman. "Simon," he said, "you see this woman? I came into your house, and you poured no water over my feet, but she has poured out her tears over my feet and wiped them away with her hair. You gave me no kiss, but she has been covering my feet with kisses ever since I came in. You did not anoint my head with oil, but she has anointed my feet with ointment. For this reason I tell you that her sins must have

been forgiven her, or she would not have shown such great love. It is the man who is forgiven little who shows little love." Then he said to her, "Your sins are forgiven." Those who were with him at table began to say to themselves, "Who is this man, that he even forgives sins?" But he said to the woman, "Your faith has saved you; go in peace" (Lk 7:36–50).

This woman virtually burst with effusive passion for Jesus. Imagine that scene in your mind's eye. The men are lounging in a circle around the common table, leaning on their left elbows, dipping their bread into the common bowls and eating. In comes a well-known woman of ill-repute who hugs Jesus' legs, cries all over his feet and wipes them dry with her long beautiful hair. Then she caresses his feet and lovingly pours oil on them. For some of her viewers, it must have been a very erotic scene!

It is remarkable that Jesus didn't become nonplussed. Somehow he managed even to keep on talking. Perhaps this was because he had been filled, caressed, and overwhelmed by a much greater passion than hers. Perhaps the passion of God had touched him so deeply that she did not in the least intimidate him.

This line of thinking seems consistent with the story he told Simon. The woman had been waiting for Jesus and, seeing that he was not honored by his host, she burst forth with her passionate offering. The setting suggests that she had had some contact with Jesus before. Perhaps she had heard him speak and seen him heal the sick. Something had happened to her through him which had put her at peace with God. It was this peace which encouraged her to display her holy passion. As his parable reveals, Jesus obviously saw that she must have been forgiven much, for through her such God-filled love and passion flowed. No one out of relationship with God could have so bravely and dramatically expressed herself. Jesus was moved by the love this woman showed him. He saw something of God in her and acknowledged it. Indeed, his goal of bringing the Kingdom was furthered by her great love and courage and he seized the opportunity to show others God's Kingdom that they too might enter.

Women and God

Unlike his contemporaries, Jesus obviously valued women highly. As we have already seen, he used them as examples in his stories (1) of those who help bring about the Kingdom (Mt 13:33), (2) of how to pray (Lk 18:1–8), (3) and of finding what was lost (Lk 15:8–10). Jesus met alone at the well that "most despicable" Samaritan woman who "had had five husbands" and through her taught her townspeople about the coming of the Kingdom (Jn 4:1–42). He was intimate friends with Martha and Mary whose brother Lazarus he raised (Jn 11:1–44).

Finally, there was the poor widow who put two small coins, the equivalent of a penny, into the temple treasury. Jesus used her as an example of one in relationship with God. He said to his disciples, "I tell you solemnly, this poor widow has put more in than all who have contributed to the treasury; for they gave from their surplus wealth, but she gave everything she possessed, all she had to live on" (Mk 12:41–44). Jesus said this after a time of watching people put money into the treasury. Of all those that he saw this widow most touched him because she did the dramatic thing. The quantity of what was given did not matter to Jesus because, as we have seen, he was not impressed with outer acts but focused on the inner significance of situations. This poor widow, seeking no recognition from others, gave all to God simply as gift. This was something Jesus could appreciate, for he himself reacted to God's call in a similar way.

Jesus thus valued women highly. He interacted with them intimately, just as he did with men. Difficult situations afforded him the opportunity to dramatize the great love of God and the great value of each woman. Intimacy with God seemed to clarify for him those social rules and values which crushed women. This intimacy also enabled him to stand against these negative values and affirm women in specific situations.

JESUS AND SINNERS

From the moment that Gabriel announced to Mary the birth of Jesus "who was to save his people from their sins" (Mt 1:21) to the very end of the Gospels, the problem of sin and forgiveness is central to Jesus' life. Jesus' teaching on sin was perhaps his most radical break with his contemporaries, for he completely overturned their notions about the nature and repercussions of sin. The religious leaders' understanding of sin determined their framework of explanation about the world and God's working in it. This framework allowed them to reject others as inappropriate, incomplete or undesirable. Jesus simply refused to accept this point of view.

Typically, the contemporaries of Jesus confessed their violations of the law to the priests, and then followed prescribed rules which brought them back into fellowship. Remember, some were excluded from fellowship *a priori* because of lineage or occupational impurity. Those who were brought back into a relationship with their community were thus restored to a situation which rejected some people as permanent outcasts. Jesus' goal was not to restore persons to fellowship in a sick society but to heal persons in order to bring about a whole society. This was but another aspect of the Kingdom. It was appropriate that people confess their sins, but only as they understood what their sins were. It seems that Jesus considered the social structure itself to be a sin when it worked against God's Kingdom. His own task was to work against all that prevented the Kingdom, and this brought conflict with the guardians of the social structure.

He said to the Pharisees:

> It is not the healthy who need the doctor, but the sick. Go and learn the meaning of the words: "What I want is mercy, not sac-

rifice" (Hos 6:6). And indeed I do not come to call the virtuous, but sinners (Mt 9:12–13).

Here Jesus took an obvious statement and applied it with stunning effect to the social situation. He accused the Pharisees of shunning the sick rather than helping them. But as we have seen, the Pharisees thought that sickness was a visitation of God for sin. It was just this perception that Jesus was trying to break by healing the sickness rather than rejecting the sinner. In the following passage, Jesus again attacked the perception that sickness and misfortune were judgments from God:

> Do you suppose these Galileans (whose blood Pilate had mingled with their sacrifices) who suffered like that were greater sinners than any other Galileans? They were not, I tell you. No; but unless you repent you will all perish as they did. Or those eighteen on whom the tower at Siloam fell and killed them? Do you suppose that they were more guilty than all the other people living in Jerusalem? They were not, I tell you. No; but unless you repent you will all perish as they did (Lk 13:2–5).

By speaking thus Jesus sought to destroy their sense of security in the centrality of sin. The issue was not sin, but how they responded to sin. Jesus compared himself to the physician who brought remedies, not judgment. The task was not to recognize the sin of another but to respond in the attitude of the Kingdom and thus help to incarnate the Kingdom.

Jesus had taught his disciples to pray that God forgive them as they forgave others. This attitude made them channels of the Kingdom. Peter pressed the issue with this question: "Lord, how often must I forgive my brother if he wrongs me? As often as seven times?" Jesus answered: "Not seven, I tell you, but seventy-seven times" (Mt 18:21–22). This response and the parable of the "unforgiving debtor" that immediately follows it demonstrate Jesus' belief in the effusiveness of God's forgiveness. So much more of a debt was owed God than to others, and that debt was forgiven. To remain in the Kingdom, to participate in the attitude of the Kingdom, one had to act as God did.

The religious leaders responded inappropriately to sin, according to Jesus, by their castigating judgment. Jesus warned them pointedly that what they did, so would God do unto them. They prided themselves on being Abraham's children, chosen to be in covenant with God, but he attacked them by saying: "If you were Abraham's children, you would do as Abraham did. . . . If God were your father, you would love me. . . . The devil is your father, and you prefer to do what your father wants" (Jn 8:39–44; see Jn 8:21–59 for the full discussion). Not only were the religious leaders wrong, according to Jesus, but their attitudes were working destruction. He brought his own view to the people:

> If you love those who love you, what thanks can you expect? Even sinners love those who love them. And if you do good to those who do good to you, what thanks can you expect? For even sinners do that much. And if you lend to those from whom you hope to receive, what thanks can you expect? Even sinners lend to sinners to get back the same amount. Instead, love your enemies and do good, and lend without any hope of return. You will have a great reward, and you will be sons of the Most High, for he himself is kind to the ungrateful and the wicked (Lk 6:32–35).

Was not Jesus saying, "What a big deal you have been making out of nothing! What you have done happens naturally. There is no righteousness in this but only blind reaction."

Jesus backed his words with actions. He called Matthew the tax collector to be one of his intimate followers (Mt 9:9). Such a call was unheard of, was totally unprecedented in Palestinian society. Tax collectors were vermin, not beloved. He ate with tax collectors and sinners, making himself continually unclean. Perhaps he did this even in his own home (Mt 9:10). He invited himself into the tax collector Zacchaeus' home (Lk 19:1). He touched lepers and others with physical ailments. He ate with Simon the Pharisee (Lk 7:36–50) whom, as we have seen in his story about the two debtors, Jesus considered a sinner. To be considered a sinner was of course an insult to Simon, but if Jesus obeyed the rules as Simon understood them he should not have eaten with Simon. But Jesus sought to bring the forgiveness of God to sinners, be they Pharisees or prostitutes. His actions were indeed consistent with his teaching for they broke with social expectations and were themselves *public* acts of intimacy. In a society so embarrassed by intimacy and sexuality, these public displays must have seemed almost pornographic to the righteous.

Jesus' expression of intimacy was consistent with his understanding of the passionate Creator Abba. Abba loved people and wanted to be intimate with them. Rather than judging those who were lost, Abba sought to bring them home. Jesus even said, in response to the accusation that he ate with sinners, that "there will be *more rejoicing* in heaven over one repentant sinner than over ninety-nine virtuous men who have no need of repentance" (Lk 15:7; emphasis mine). Though there was a tongue in cheek quality to his response in that *he* did not consider the scribes and Pharisees to be truly virtuous, there was also an invitation to them to see the forgiveness of God who positively rejoiced when one returned home. Jesus' own reaction to the oppressed, the broken, and the lost who were found was this same joy. The table fellowship he shared with sinners was indeed the feast of the Kingdom.

THE DISCIPLES

One would expect great intimacy between Jesus and his small band of followers who had left their professions to travel and work with him. A person like Jesus, who showed so much courageous intimacy in public, would have deep friendships with his closest companions with whom he spent so much time. He taught them, talked things over with them, poured out his heart to them about what he was to suffer, argued and was angry with them.

Peter, James and John seemed to be part of an inner, more intimate circle with him. These three he brought with him to the mountain for the transfiguration, and these same he brought closer to him when he went to pray in Gethsemane. One disciple (presumably John) was called the "one Jesus loved." Such a nickname or title would most likely arise out of observation. Perhaps he stood closer to John, talked quietly with him, put his arm around him more than the others, and looked to him with more love in his eyes.

The Gospels suggest that Jesus and his disciples were an intimate group. This was all the more likely because they perceived themselves as a little group in the midst of a larger enemy. They knew that the religious leaders wanted to destroy them. The fact that there was a tax collector among the little band made this even more true. He certainly did not gain favor with the Romans by having a Zealot among his group. And it is easy to imagine that when inner tension moved through the group, vigorous and crisp arguments took place between Matthew the tax collector and Simon the Zealot.

Jesus' followers were everyday people, drawn from Jewish life. Probably he would have accepted a Pharisee as a follower if one had so desired. Remember (Jn 3:1ff) that Nicodemus the Pharisee sought out Jesus' teaching by night and that Jesus told him what he must do. But no Pharisee seemed able or willing to join that motley band.

This rough-hewn group of men, Jesus' closest friends, were exposed to more of him than anyone else. When the time came for Jesus to die it was to them that he turned for human support. Before that fateful journey to Gethsemane, he shared with them a last meal, the great Jewish feast of Passover—and this with the knowledge that the angel of death would not pass him by.

The Gospels report the first celebration of the Eucharist at that dinner. Jesus had read the signs and knew that he must die, but there burned within him a deep longing to share the full richness of the

Kingdom with his followers, that they might take all that he had done and said deep into their hearts and be filled with it and transformed. Not much more than this celebration of Eucharist is reported in Matthew, Mark or Luke's account of the Last Supper. Each leaves the reader with a feeling of poignancy for this human being whose love brought him to the narrow door of death.

John's Gospel, however, contains an elaborate statement filling five chapters (13–17). Much of what is written there is perhaps a reflection of the early Church, which was itself suffering persecution. Nevertheless, four different aspects of Jesus' view of intimacy are found in these five chapters: (1) Jesus' intimacy with God, (2) his intimacy with his disciples, (3) their intimacy with God, and (4) their intimacy among themselves.

Intimacy with God

How did Jesus view his relationship with God? He said to the disciples: "If you know me, you know my Father too." Philip said that they would be satisfied if they could see the Father and Jesus responded, "To have seen me is to have seen the Father. . . . It is the Father, living in me, who is doing this work" (Jn 14:7–10). In other words, so intimately involved was Jesus with God that everything he did was an expression of God's work. At the same time, he knew that he was going to his death and that the political and spiritual powers gathering around him would frighten his friends away. Only God would be with him. As he said, "The time will come—in fact it has come already—when you will be scattered, each going his own way and leaving me alone. And yet I am not alone because the Father is with me" (16:32). So deeply and intimately present was God to him that even the threat of death did not negate his love for God or for his friends. A person would be easily forgiven who said in such a situation: "If you desert me now, you are not my friends nor ever have been." But Jesus expressed just the opposite feeling toward them.

Intimacy with the Disciples

Several statements in these five chapters show Jesus' great feelings for his friends.

(1) *My little children,* I shall not be with you much longer (13:33; emphasis mine).

(2) I will not leave you *orphans;* I will come back to you (14:18; emphasis mine).

(3) I'm going to prepare a place for you, and after I've gone and prepared you a place, I shall return to take you with me (14:2–3).

(4) I shall not call you servants anymore. . . . I call you friends (15:15).

(5) As the Father has loved me, so I have loved you (15:9).

(6) (In his prayer to God:) with me in them and you in me may they be so completely one that the world will realize that it was you who sent me and that I have loved them as much as you have loved me (17:23).

(7) Love one another as I have loved you (13:34).

(8) I am the vine, you are the branches (15:1).

The vine is perhaps the most intimate of plants, growing over itself, into and around itself, intricately connected but needing to be pruned so it does not choke itself or stunt its own growth. Jesus' image was the perfect expression of intimacy. So connected were they to him that he supplied their nourishment and spiritual sustenance. But he was leaving them, and though he would return, he saw that it was necessary for them to establish their own relationship with God, to find God in their own hearts and not just in his presence. This was an act of great emptying, for Jesus said something like: "*Your own* relationship with God is crucial and you have found that through me. You must see that God loves you for yourselves and that you are yourselves connected to God."

The Disciples and God

Jesus gave them some clues to understand the paradox he had presented. "The Advocate, the Holy Spirit, whom the Father will send in my name, will teach you everything" (14:26). Jesus' uneducated followers would be taught by the Spirit just as he had been taught in the desert and in prayer. Jesus saw that what he wished for would happen, that God would come straight to them *because* he loved them. They were perhaps too dependent on Jesus who wished them to be connected to the God of whom he said: "The Father is greater than I am" (14:28). After having told Philip that "to see me is to see the Father," Jesus showed his own humility and submitted to God. But he also brought into clear view the paradox so well illustrated in the image of the vine: "On that day you will understand that I am in my Father and you in me and I in you" (14:19).

The Disciples Themselves

Jesus gave the disciples one great command which, simple as it sounds, was his ultimate teaching on intimacy: "This is my commandment: love one another, as I have loved you" (15:12). Reflecting on all that Jesus had said before, we can see that the accomplishment of this command was obviously no mean task, particularly as we remember that he also said, as he walked to face his own death, "A man can have no greater love than to lay down his life for his friends" (15:13). Loving one another in such a way is the deepest and most difficult task. In his last words before going to the garden, Jesus expressed in a prayer to God the truth which made possible his simple and impossible command: "I have made your name known to them and will continue to make it known, so that the love with which you loved me may be in them, and so that I may be in them" (17:26).

This great mystical statement contains a deep truth of connection and intimacy. As we have seen, Jesus' own experience with God was passionately intimate. He had discovered that God wanted the Kingdom to come in daily life and had made a commitment to bring the news of the Kingdom to others. Both Jesus and God seemed deeply concerned that others reach the Kingdom because it was diminished by the absence of those who were not there. In his life and work, Jesus had shared with the disciples his own deep experiences of God and the Kingdom. He saw that God was making this same intimacy available to his friends. As they came to experience the depth of God's intimacy, they, God and Jesus would all be deeply connected because the gift of this deep experience of the Kingdom was what Jesus' whole life was about.

8.

Anger

That Jesus was a person who loved deeply does not surprise us, for all of us have learned that the center of Christianity is love. More startling, however, is the image of the angry Jesus. It troubles us to realize that he was quite as capable of anger as of love. This somehow makes it more difficult to control him; it makes him seem more dangerous and more human.

The Gospels report literally dozens of times when Jesus was angry.* This should not surprise us, because when a person is threatened, the sympathetic nervous system automatically prepares for "fight or flight." This is a very old instinctual response that is necessary to preserve the organism in dangerous situations. Perhaps there is a particular person in your own life at the present that you hate or fear. Think about what that person did or does to make you feel this way. As you continue to think about that person you may notice that you feel different than you did a moment ago: your heart beats a little faster and you breathe a little faster; you feel a rush of

*Some examples of Jesus' anger are found in: Mt 5:22; 5:25; 6:5; 11:20; 12:34ff; 15:1ff; 16:21; 17:15; 18:5; 18:23; 19:13; 21:12ff; 21:18; 22:15ff; 23:1ff; 23:28ff; 23:33ff; 27:12; Mk 2:6; 3:5; 7:6; 7:14; 8:17; 9:42; 10:5; 10:13; 11:12; 11:15; 12:15; 12:24; 12:38; 14:48; Lk 9:41; 10:13; 11:37; 12:1; 12:3; 12:54; 13:45; 19:45.

energy. Perhaps you feel ready to run or are firmly planted where you are. You may be clenching your fists or, if you are very upset, your palms may be sweating. You probably also feel angry and/or anxious. These are manifestations of the fight or flight response, and you have been able to elicit them just by imagining the earlier situation.

Of course Jesus also experienced the fight or flight response. It is not surprising that he found himself in many tense situations because his message threatened the status quo. The very nature of his message frequently constellated the fight or flight response in others. The Pharisees and scribes in particular were often in a complete rage about him. They felt attacked and threatened by him and wanted to do away with him, which is simply the fight aspect of this response. When the Gerasenes asked him in fear to leave their country after he had cured the demoniac (Lk 8:37) they were exhibiting the flight aspect of the response.

Though it is important as a survival mechanism, the fight or flight response is basically automatic. In life-threatening situations it is indispensable, but any situation which is *perceived* as threatening (such as a job interview or an argument with one's spouse) elicits the response. The person becomes angry and/or afraid and is often unable to deal creatively with the (non-life-threatening) problem at hand. Rather the person's inclination is to fight the "attacker" (even if a potential boss, spouse, or friend) or to flee. Jesus did not deny the value of this response. Indeed he must have had a deep experience of it. He could not have had his life completely overturned without feeling anger or anxiety; nor could he spend forty days in the presence of God without quivering a bit.

The response has real value, but Jesus knew that as the *final* determinant of behavior, it was destructive and led to disharmony and hatred. His teachings show how he solved the "fight or flight" problem, but in order to better understand these teachings we must examine his own relationship to anger. To this end, we will first use imagination to consider Jesus' struggle to understand his anger.

Then we will explore his anger at the religious leaders and the society, at demons, and at his own disciples, and finally examine his treatment of anger in his stories.

A FANTASY

In Chapter 3, we examined Jesus' teaching about the Kingdom. As we considered then, his insights were hard-won through his own struggle in the desert. We will now use imagination to re-enter the desert so that we may examine Jesus' struggle to understand anger.

Perhaps like Moses Jesus had a time when he argued with God. "But they won't listen to me, a carpenter. My own family doesn't listen to me. *Your* own people have not listened to the prophets you have sent them. How can I possibly get your message across to such stubborn people?"

Voice of God
(V):   By first giving the message to yourself.

Jesus (J):   How do I do that?

V: First see the plank in your own eye. You are angry with your family for not accepting you. How can you expect them to get over their anger if you cannot get over yours?

J: Yes, I see that. It's hard to get over this anger. But my anger is justified. You've called me to do your work.

V: Yes, dear Son, but they feel their anger is justified. In their minds, you've deserted them.

J: It's this that angers me most.

V: Listen and I'll explain. Anger itself is good; it warns you of dangerous situations; it tells you something is wrong. It's natural and healthy. But the Evil One takes anger which is valuable and makes it the final value. This tricks people into letting the anger make the final decision. Thus the Zealots want to destroy the Romans and justify themselves by their anger. Thus your people hate the Samaritans and get caught in their anger. But anger is not the final value. It is but a messenger. Listen then to the messenger but do not think that he is king.

J: I'm to let anger be, then move beyond it?

V: Yes, my Son, anger *protects* you but finally it separates you from others. You cannot deny it, for that only opens you to sickness and despair. See the hardness of those caught by their anger: the Zealots at Rome, the Pharisees at rule-breakers, the Jews and Samaritans at each other. Anger unresolved turns to hatred, and hatred finally solves nothing. See what a disaster the world is. If I were like these people, I would be full of hatred, for they block the coming of the Kingdom.

J: But you don't hate them, do you?

V: No, I love them. I rain on the wicked and the good alike.

J: How can you love those who are enemies of the Kingdom?

V: I see that they're stuck in their anger rather than using it for immediate protection. They are una-

ble to recognize that the feared danger can be resolved. This is a trick of the Evil One. You need
a trick of your own against the Evil One. What
you must do is accept anger as a proper expression
of your dissatisfaction with a world which ex-
cludes the Kingdom. Let the others see your anger—so caught are they in anger that it excels in
getting their attention. And then, dear Son, do
this with your anger. Let it dissolve as does the
smoke of a fire. Let it be a sacrifice to me. Let
them feel the heat of your anger and then the
warmth of the Kingdom. It is your anger which
burns the fire and love which welcomes them.
This is a difficult request, even impossible, if you
yourself do not already feel the truth of it. Bring
your anger to me; put it on a purifying fire. See
that I do not want destruction but rather a feast.
Their ways lead to destruction. Isaiah has said it:
the lion shall lie down with the lamb. This is the
secret you are to bring: Forgiveness goes where
anger cannot. Anger points out the sore, forgiveness heals it. No outer show can change this fact.
If you forgive, you will feel my forgiveness and
this is entry into the Kingdom. If you love, you
will feel my love which is the event of the Kingdom. If you die to self, a greater life can happen
which is the Kingdom. Doing this, you will have
removed the plank from your own eye and will see
life as it is. The central goal of life is not avoidance of sin, but seeking relationship. This can
happen only as you step out of anger with your
brother and make up with him. Forgive once, accept his forgiveness if it is needed, forgive each
time, for that is the nature of the Kingdom. But
the one who does not forgive, that one cannot find
his way here. Forgiveness is the key.

Some such message from God may have come, leaving Jesus to come to grips with it. Perhaps his mind turned to the scribes and Pharisees with whom he would battle, and he was angry at them for blocking the Kingdom with their rules. But then he felt a shift in awareness and forgave them, hoping that they would find the way. He recalled his family and friends in Nazareth and was angry that they had made his own decision more difficult, but he forgave them because they had been trapped by an old view of him. He felt anger toward the Zealots, the Romans, the Sadducees—all of whom blocked the love of the Kingdom. Feeling that love himself, he forgave them that they might enter the Kingdom.

Jesus felt anger as does anyone else but he found a dramatic and creative solution to it. We see this solution in the teachings which grew out of his own experience. He recognized enemies but called for a *conscious* response to them rather than an automatic one. He accepted anger but moved beyond it because *by itself* it wasn't creative. He did not ask the impossible by saying: "*Deny* that person is your enemy." Rather he met the situation head on: "See that person as enemy and come to terms with him or her. When you do, you will see what I have discovered about sinners, tax collectors and prostitutes: that they are not enemy first but people, and that as people they are loved and forgiven. By loving the enemy, you learn to love in yourself what you most hate and defend against." By loving his enemies, Jesus faced with love and forgiveness the part of himself that struggled against the Kingdom. He won this struggle because God's words to him proved to be true; forgiveness is the key and there is no forgiveness until enmity is acknowledged and transformed.

SCRIBES, PHARISEES, SOCIETY

Jesus' relationship with the Jewish religious leaders was anything but cordial. He had particular trouble with the scribes and

Pharisees. The Gospel narrative is packed with arguments and debates which he had with them and traps they set for him. Perhaps Jesus had this special difficulty with them because the scribes and Pharisees had so much to lose by heeding his words; they refused to be brought into an awareness of the Kingdom by the stories, teachings or healings because these threatened their social position and their view of themselves.

The Gospels are rife with examples of the harsh words Jesus used to describe the religious leaders to the crowds:

> Be careful not to parade your good deeds before men to attract their notice. . . . This is what the hypocrites do in the synagogues and in the streets to win men's admiration. I tell you solemnly, they have had their reward (Mt 6:1–3).

> And when you pray, do not imitate the hypocrites; they love to say their prayers standing up in the synagogues and at the street corners for people to see them. I tell you solemnly, they have had their reward (Mt 6:5).

> When you fast do not put on a gloomy look as the hypocrites do; they pull long faces to let men know they are fasting. I tell you solemnly, they have had their reward (Mt 6:16).

> Beware of the scribes who like to walk about in long robes and love to be greeted obsequiously in the market squares, to take the front seats in the synagogues and the places of honor at banquets, who swallow the property of widows, while making a great show of lengthy prayers. The more severe will be the sentence they receive (Lk 20:46–47).

The primary problem Jesus had with the scribes and Pharisees was their self-righteousness, their seeking after *personal* recognition. The danger of such behavior is that one's reward so often matches one's behavior. The scribes and Pharisees successfully achieved outer recognition but this, according to Jesus, missed the point, which is the incarnation of the Kingdom in daily life. Not only did the scribes and Pharisees endanger themselves with this self-seeking approach; they also worked *against* the coming of the Kingdom.

Jesus called them hypocrites because they thought themselves righteous before God and sought personal recognition under false pretenses. To be called hypocrites is a great insult, particularly to persons like the scribes and Pharisees who base their self-justification on literal fulfillment of the law. Jesus was again trying to shake them out of their trance so that they and others might see that inner motivation was more important than ritual obedience of the rules. In one situation the Pharisees were upset with Jesus because his followers did not follow the prescribed washing ritual before eating. Jesus answered:

> And why do you break away from the commandment of God for the sake of your tradition? For God said: "Do your duty to your father and mother," and "Anyone who curses father or mother must be put to death." But you say, "If anyone says to his father or mother: 'Anything I have that I might have used to help you is dedicated to God,' he is rid of his duty to his father or mother." [Property dedicated in this way could not be passed to another person.] In this way you have made God's word null and void by means of your tradition. Hypocrites! It was you Isaiah meant when he so rightly prophesied:
>> This people honors me only with lip service,
>> while their hearts are far from me.
>> The worship they offer me is worthless;
>> the doctrines they teach are only human regulations
> (Mt 15:3–9).

Again notice how he insulted them, accusing them of working directly against God. He then said to the people near him:

> Listen, and understand. What goes into the mouth does not make a man unclean; it is what comes out of the mouth that makes him unclean (Mt 15:10–11).

With these words he overturned the measure of acceptability used by the scribes and Pharisees, just as he would overturn the tables in the temple. Listen to what he said to the scribes and Pharisees at other times:

> You are the very ones that pass yourselves off as virtuous in people's sight, but God knows your hearts. For what is thought highly of by men is loathsome in the sight of God (Lk 16:15).

> Brood of vipers, how can your speech be good when you are evil? For a man's words flow out of what fills his heart. A good man draws good things from his store of goodness; a bad man draws bad things from his store of badness. So I tell you this, that for every unfounded word men utter they will answer on judgment day, since it is by your words you will be acquitted, and by your words condemned (Mt 12:34–37).

> Serpents, brood of vipers, how can you escape being condemned to hell? (Mt 23:33).

Clearly Jesus responded angrily to the scribes and Pharisees. As we have seen, this was for two main reasons. First, they blocked themselves from entering the Kingdom by their attitude. Second, because they were so powerful, the people listened to them, followed their teaching and thus were also prevented from entering the Kingdom. For Jesus, to whom the Kingdom was central and ultimate, this was unbearable; quite naturally it evoked the fight response in him. Anything that barred the way to the Kingdom must be met directly. As he said, "He who is not with me is against me" (Mt 12:30). The scribes and Pharisees definitely were not with him. It is written in several places in the Gospels that he made them furious and they plotted to destroy him.

In the following account from Luke, Jesus exploded with anger against them. A Pharisee had invited Jesus to dine at his house. When Jesus sat down at table, the Pharisee was surprised that Jesus had not first washed. Jesus answered him:

"Oh, you Pharisees! You clean the outside of cup and plate, while inside yourselves you are filled with extortion and wickedness. Fools! Did not he who made the outside make the inside too? Instead, give alms from what you have and then indeed everything will be clean for you. But alas for you Pharisees! You who pay your tithe of mint and rue and all sorts of garden herbs and overlook justice and the love of God! These you should have practiced, without leaving the others undone. Alas for you Pharisees who like taking the seats of honor in the synagogues and being greeted obsequiously in the market squares! Alas for you, because you are like the unmarked tombs that men walk on without knowing it!"

A lawyer then spoke up. "Master," he said, "when you speak like this you insult us too." "Alas for you lawyers also," he replied, "because you load on men burdens that are unendurable, burdens that you yourselves do not move a finger to lift.

"Alas for you who build the tombs of the prophets, the men your ancestors killed! In this way you both witness what your ancestors did and approve it; they did the killing, you do the building.

"And that is why the Wisdom of God said, 'I will send them prophets and apostles; some they will slaughter and persecute, so that this generation will have to answer for every prophet's blood that has been shed since the foundation of the world, from the blood of Abel to the blood of Zechariah, who was murdered between the altar and the sanctuary.' Yes, I tell you, this generation will have to answer for it all.

"Alas for you lawyers who have taken away the key of

knowledge! You have not gone in yourselves, and have prevented others going in who wanted to."

When he left the house, the scribes and the Pharisees began a furious attack on him and tried to force answers from him on innumerable questions, setting traps to catch him out in something he might say (Lk 11:39–54).

Jesus pulled no punches in this devastating attack. It is no wonder that the scribes and Pharisees responded as they did, for it is the natural course to fight or flee when so attacked, and thus it was natural that they wanted to destroy him.

Not surprisingly, this anger toward the scribes and Pharisees was also occasionally directed toward the larger population.

> What description can I find for this generation? It is like children shouting to each other as they sit in the market place:
> "We played the pipes for you,
>   and you wouldn't dance;
> we sang dirges,
>   and you wouldn't be mourners."
> For John came, neither eating nor drinking, and they say, "He is possessed." The son of Man came, eating and drinking, and they say, "Look, a glutton and a drunkard, a friend of tax collectors and sinners." Yet wisdom has been proved right by her actions (Mt 11:16–19).

John was rejected because he didn't dance, Jesus because he did. Thus the people had successfully shut off any possibility for insight and change.

His anger then turned on the towns where he had worked miracles, because they had refused to repent:

> Alas for you, Chorazin! Alas for you, Bethsaida! For if the miracles done in you had been done in Tyre and Sidon, they would

have repented long ago in sackcloth and ashes. And still, I tell
you that it will not go as hard on judgment day with Tyre and
Sidon as with you. And as for you, Capernaum, did you want to
be exalted as high as heaven? You shall be thrown down to hell.
For if the miracles done in you had been done in Sodom, it would
have been standing yet. And still, I tell you that it will not go
as hard with the land of Sodom on judgment day as with you (Mt
11:21–24).

Jerusalem, Jerusalem, you that kill the prophets and stone those
who are sent to you! How often have I longed to gather your children, as a hen gathers her chicks under her wings, and you refused! So be it! Your house will be left to you desolate, for, I
promise, you shall not see me anymore until you say: "Blessings
on him who comes in the name of the Lord" (Mt 23:37–39).

The coming of the Kingdom was being blocked on all sides and his
anger came forth appropriately. That most famous of angry outbursts, the expulsion of the dealers from the temple, simply is a specific example of the general situation.

So they reached Jerusalem and he went into the temple and began driving out those who were selling and buying there; he upset the tables of the money changers and the chairs of those who
were selling pigeons. Nor would he allow anyone to carry anything through the temple. And he taught them and said, "Does
not Scripture say: My house will be called a house of prayer for
all the peoples? But you have turned it into a robbers' den." This
came to the ears of the chief priests and the scribes, and they
tried to find some way of doing away with him; they were afraid
of him because the people were carried away by his teaching.
And when evening came he went out of the city (Mk 11:15–19).

This dramatic scene shows much about Jesus' anger. First of all,
he was enraged because the money changing practices were essen-

tially extortionary. Only Galilean or temple currency was accepted to pay the required temple tax and to purchase animals for sacrifice, because other currencies were unclean. With their high rate of exchange the money changers "robbed" the pilgrims who had come to pay their tax and to offer sacrifice to God. For example, only animals without blemish could be sacrificed at the altar. Since the authorities determined whether an animal was blemished, almost no animal purchased outside was ruled admissible. And the temple price for animals was sometimes twenty times as high as the market price in the city outside.

Second, animal sacrifice was again an *outer* ritual with no necessary connection to the person's inner condition. By sacrificing an animal, the person had fulfilled his obligation. This was to Jesus hypocritical, for it was what came from *within* the heart which was important.

The primary goal of money changing was profit, not worship of God. This, obviously, went against Jesus' notion of the coming of the Kingdom. The actual selling took place in the court of the Gentiles. The temple was arranged so that a series of courts led into the Holy Place. Beyond the court of the Gentiles were the separate courts of women, Israelites and priests. The temple was to be a "house of prayer for all the peoples," and yet the court of Gentiles, the only place in the temple accessible to the Gentiles, was virtually a madhouse, with screaming money changers and bleating animals making it impossible for a person to pray. Jesus' rage was that God had again been denied to the unacceptable. True to his own belief that God welcomed *everyone* to the Kingdom, he turned over the tables and cleared the area so that the true function of the temple could be accomplished. The situation in the temple, itself a manifestation of the general situation of society, was intolerable to Jesus. He could not just let it be. He had to leave the temple or confront the problem directly. His behavior simply shows how important the Kingdom of God was to him and how little validity he attached to the opinion of the authorities.

DEMONS

Jesus' anger was not reserved for persons who kept themselves and others from the Kingdom. Again and again he expressed irritation at demons who had possessed human beings. He was angry with them for two reasons. First, even more than other illnesses, demon possession separated the person from the Kingdom of God. The possessed person was out of relationship with God and further, because of social rules, was also out of relationship with others. As discussed in Chapter 5, sin was considered the cause of illness, and this made it especially difficult for the sick person to be healed.

Second, Jesus rebuked the demons for a specific reason. On at least three occasions (Mk 1:25; 1:34; 3:11) the demons "recognized" Jesus and called out words like: "I know who you are: the Holy One of God." Jesus answered: "Keep quiet! Come out of him!" For some reason, Jesus did not want to be made known. As we have suggested earlier, he probably did not want to be seen as the Messiah because of the meanings attached to that word by the people, and because he wanted the emphasis to be on the Kingdom, not on himself.

That the demons "recognized" him is a very curious thing. If, as believed in those days, demons are autonomous spiritual beings, then they might have been able to "see" Jesus differently than could human beings. This type of thinking stretches modern minds, for we can hardly imagine demons as autonomous entities but rather prefer to consider them as "complexes" or "split-off personalities," autonomous in the sense of not being under ego control but certainly not real in themselves.

Jesus' experience in the desert suggests his own attitude. At the end of the forty days, Satan or the "Adversary" tempted Jesus to take personal advantage of his newly acquired power and insights. After dealing with the temptations, Jesus finally said, "Be off, Satan! For Scripture says: 'You must worship the Lord your God, and serve him alone.' " Again, a modern interpretation might see Jesus here mastering his selfish motives, but Jesus saw it as this and more. For him, there was a negative, destructive force in life hell-bent on sabotaging the coming of the Kingdom. Human pride, lust for power and hatred were not sufficient to explain the depth of evil in life. Something suprapersonal seemed to entice and activate these human proclivities. It was this greater-than-human negative force which exploited human selfishness and pride. Only by acknowledging its reality and confronting it directly could one overcome it and enter into the Kingdom. It was this negative power which controlled the scribes and Pharisees in their pride, separation and selfishness. The scribes, the Pharisees, and even society itself were not the principal enemy of the Kingdom. Rather, it was this destructive force, called Satan here but known by other names, that Jesus battled. Jesus saw the struggle occurring on the cosmic level; it is no wonder that he snapped at the religious officials in an attempt to wake them up.

THE DISCIPLES

Nor were his disciples immune to his anger. Here too his anger was usually precipitated by forces working against the coming of the Kingdom. The basic reason for Jesus' annoyance with his disciples was that they too failed to understand him. When Jesus came down from the transfiguration and was presented with the epileptic boy that his disciples had been unable to heal, he said, "You faithless generation. How much longer must I be with you? How much longer must I put up with you?" (Mk 9:19). Obviously some of his exasperation was with his disciples who had failed to heal the boy. His outburst was quite natural because their inability to heal represented to him that the Kingdom wasn't coming rapidly into being without him. This distressed him, for he knew he wouldn't always be there to "save the day." The disciples needed to get a better handle on the healing process themselves. Notice that after expressing his anger, he moved beyond it and healed the boy. His anger here was that lack of faith worked against the Kingdom.

Their lack of faith again angered him when he told them to beware of the yeast of the scribes and Pharisees. The disciples took him quite literally because they had forgotten to bring bread with them. Exasperated, Jesus responded, "Men of little faith, why are you talking among yourselves about having no bread? Do you not yet understand? Do you not remember the five loaves for the five thousand . . . and the seven loaves for the four thousand and the number of baskets you collected? How could you fail to understand that I was not talking about bread? What I said was: Beware of the yeast of the Pharisees and scribes" (Mt 16:5–11). It annoyed Jesus that his followers so often missed the deeper meaning of his sayings and actions.

Miracles

This brings us to the miracle stories in which Jesus expressed anger at his disciples' lack of faith. The miracles seem to be particularly important to Jesus not because they were astounding in themselves but rather because they were events of the Kingdom. His disciples' attitude to some of the miracles showed that they still misunderstood the Kingdom.

We will briefly consider two of these miracles.

In the story presently under examination, the reported miracle was the feeding of the multitudes. What miracle occurred? Did Jesus spontaneously produce thousands of fish and loaves? Did he take the few loaves he had and share them with others, thus inspiring those who had food hidden to bring it forth and share it with each other? The Gospels are not clear about this. The second possibility would have been in itself a great miracle, demonstrating Jesus' ability to evoke intimacy, and an example of the Kingdom in action.

Other reported miracles do not submit so easily to "natural" explanations. Consider the calming of the storm:

> With the coming of evening that same day, he said to them, "Let us cross over to the other side." And leaving the crowd behind they took him, just as he was, in the boat; and there were

other boats with him. Then it began to blow a gale and the
waves were breaking into the boat so that it was almost
swamped. But he was in the stern, his head on the cushion,
asleep. They woke him and said to him, "Master, do you not
care? We are going down!" And he woke up and rebuked the
wind and said to the sea, "Quiet now! Be calm!" And the wind
dropped, and all was calm again. Then he said to them, "Why
are you so frightened? How is it that you have no faith?" They
were filled with awe and said to one another, "Who can this be?
Even the wind and the sea obey him" (Mk 4:35–41).

To actually believe this story leaves us as astounded as the disciples, for we too lack the faith to believe that such a thing is possible. Two similar examples from other sources may help us here. The
first story is about the rainmaker. It seems that a great drought had
come to a certain province of China. Catholic processions, Protestant
prayers and Chinese guns all attempted to frighten away the demons
of the drought. Finally the Chinese decided to fetch the rainmaker,
and soon a wizened old man from another province appeared. Immediately he asked for a quiet place and went into seclusion for three
days. On the fourth day a great storm occurred. A curious Western
observer asked him how he had done this and he refused to take credit
for it. Rather he said he came from a country where things were in
order, but this place was out of order. He thus needed to be by himself to get back into the natural order of things and when that happened, he said, the rains naturally came.

In the second story, Hosteen Klah, a Navaho medicine man was
traveling with a family across the desert. Suddenly about one half
mile ahead of them a tornado appeared headed directly toward them.
The others recoiled in fright but it was too late to escape. Klah
walked toward the tornado, picking up herbs and chewing them as
he walked. All at once he raised both arms and began chanting
loudly. The tornado stood still, then broke apart, the top half going
in one direction, the bottom in another. His explanation of this re-

markable event was simply that the earth spirit is stronger than the wind spirit.

Jesus would have recognized that these two men had great faith which enabled them to stand up to the natural situation. His own followers, however, did not see that they had the same power as he had. Perhaps he thought that just one of them could have handled the situation so that he could get his much needed sleep. This in itself was a great act of faith on his part, for he obviously believed they could have this great power if only they believed. His annoyance came because their vision of themselves was too small.

Two Other Situations

The disciples were consistent to the end. In John's account of the Last Supper (Jn 14:8–9) Philip asked Jesus to let them see the Father so that they could be satisfied. Jesus answered, "Have I been with you all this time, Philip, and you still do not know me? To have seen me is to have seen the Father." Again Jesus and his followers were out of synch. This is another example of the disciples' misunderstanding of Jesus' desire to bring the Kingdom. This difficult passage from John seems to express Jesus' belief that he was so attuned and committed to God's purpose that he was facilitating the coming of the Kingdom. If Philip and the other disciples could not see the Kingdom or the Father in Jesus' actions, they had no perception of who the Father was. This naturally angered Jesus because it indicated that his followers had again missed the point that he was so God-centered, so committed to bringing God's will, that God was, as it were, acting directly through him.

In another well-known situation some children wanted to be near Jesus, to hold him and play with him, but the disciples tried to send them away. Mark tells us that Jesus was indignant and said to them:

> "Let the little children come to me; do not stop them; for it is
> to such as these that the Kingdom of God belongs. I tell you sol-

emnly, anyone who does not welcome the Kingdom of God like a little child will never enter it." Then he put his arms around them, laid his hands on them and gave them his blessing (Mk 10:14–16).

The open attitude of the children was what was needed to enter the Kingdom. Jesus' anger at the disciples was twofold: (1) for sending away those who already were available to the Kingdom, and (2) for not seeing the openness of children, which was necessary for *them* if they were to enter the Kingdom. The disciples, like everyone else, kept missing the clues to the Kingdom.

Peter

Peter was particularly close to Jesus and quite often received his anger. When Peter asked Jesus to explain a parable to them Jesus not surprisingly responded: "Do even you not yet understand?" (Mt 15:15–16). Later, after Jesus told his disciples of his upcoming death, Peter took him aside. "Heaven preserve you, Lord," he said. "This must not happen to you." Jesus replied: "Get behind me, Satan! You are an obstacle in my path, because the way you think is not God's way but man's" (16:21–23). Peter seems to have hit a sore spot. Jesus responded to him as he had to the tempter in the desert. Peter quite naturally did not want Jesus to suffer and die and spoke accordingly, but Jesus needed to shout down the temptation so that he could do God's will. Again, the Kingdom came first in Jesus' eyes. If his death facilitated the coming of the Kingdom, he would willingly die. Like any other human being, he wanted to live, and this desire for life sometimes directly challenged the work of the Kingdom. How surprised Peter must have been at this response to his expression of concern!

At the Last Supper, Jesus enacted a parable for his disciples by acting as servant and washing their feet:

> He came to Simon Peter, who said to him, "Lord, are you going to wash my feet?" Jesus answered, "At the moment you do not

know what I am doing, but later you will understand."
"Never!" said Peter. "You shall never wash my feet." Jesus replied, "If I do not wash you, you can have nothing in common
with me." "Then, Lord," said Simon Peter, "not only my feet,
but my hands and my head as well" (Jn 13:6–9).

Peter could not at first picture his master being the servant. This was
an unheard of act in Palestinian society. Peter again quite naturally
"politely" refused the gesture. Perhaps he even felt that he should do
this to indicate that he saw Jesus as his master. But, true to form,
Jesus shocked him, and at the thought of losing him, Peter opened
himself willingly to Jesus the servant.

There is also the story of Peter stepping out on the water to go
to Jesus who had been walking across the lake (Mt 14:22–23). When
Peter lost heart and began to sink, Jesus put out his hand and helped
him. "Man of little faith," he said, "why did you doubt?" This remarkable question shows how much faith Jesus had in Peter. How
else can we explain his annoyance with Peter who had attempted (and
briefly succeeded at) what was impossible?

STORIES IN THE KINGDOM

Jesus' anger sometimes entered his stories of the Kingdom. In
the parable of the unforgiving debtor (Mt 18:23–35) Jesus told of the
king who forgave a man his enormous debt after the man begged for
mercy. This servant then went out and met another servant who owed
him a very small debt. When the second servant pleaded with him
for mercy, he wouldn't listen and threw the man into prison. On
hearing of this the master called the wicked servant and told him that
he was bound to pity this fellow servant just as the king had pitied
him. In his anger the king handed him over to the torturers until he
should pay all his debt. Then Jesus said: "And that is how my heav-
enly Father will deal with you unless you each forgive your brother
from your heart."

In another parable, Jesus told of a man who went abroad and left three servants in charge of some of his money. The first two invested their money and the third buried his money in the ground. When the master returned, he commended the first two for their wise investments but he was enraged with the third, blaming him for not at least depositing the money in the bank and drawing interest. His final words about this third servant were: "As for this good-for-nothing servant, throw him out into the dark, where there will be weeping and gnashing of teeth" (Mt 25:14–30).

Both parables suggest that Jesus saw God as one who could become angry under certain conditions. In the first parable, the king who was an image of God forgave the enormous debt of the servant who in turn put his fellow servant in prison for the debt he owed. We might rather expect the first servant to have been so grateful that he would have said to the other: "Celebrate with me, man! The king has wiped the slate clean! Why, the debt you owe me is as nothing to what I have been given, and as of this moment consider it cancelled!" The wickedness of the fellow is that he could not celebrate the great event which had occurred to him. So locked in his own life was he that he could not be broken open to bring the same forgiveness to another. The king's rage came after he had done *everything*, forgiven all. The man was sent to prison to repay his bill because he had no understanding of forgiveness and could not use it to his spiritual advantage.

The "culprit" of the second parable gave back to the master exactly what was given to him. The poor fellow missed the point altogether that the master was entrusting him with his goods. *His* view of the master was that it was better to play it safe than to use the money and perhaps lose some of it. The master's anger came because the servant totally misunderstood him. The master did not want given back to him the same piece of money; rather he wanted to *involve* and engage the servant in the affairs of his life but the servant essentially refused. Even his perception of the master didn't excuse him, for as the master said he could have at least put the money in the bank. Just giving back to God what had been given was not good enough. What then would have happened to this servant had he lost all the master's funds? Consider the story of the prodigal for a possible answer to that question. God seems to seek involvement rather than increase in value per se. The servant who did not risk anything lost everything—a terrifying thought.

Anger then was an integral aspect of the personality and life of Jesus. This natural response was a valuable learning tool for him. He used his anger as a marker that showed him when something or someone worked against the Kingdom. Expressing his anger allowed him to call attention to these obstacles blocking the Kingdom. But Jesus' intimate understanding of God moved him beyond his anger to a desire to bring the Kingdom to everyone. He was always ready to help persons break through the attitudes that kept them separated from God, and his anger was one of the ways he facilitated this breakthrough to the Kingdom.

9.

Courage

From the moment Jesus met John at the River Jordan until his death by crucifixion the Gospels tell an ongoing story of courage. To fulfill his unique destiny and to answer the intimations of his soul required strength, fortitude and bravery. Jesus could not have accomplished what he did if he had lacked courage. The forces of society worked against him, rules and expectations attempted to deaden his message, and the deep destructiveness in life assaulted and finally killed him. Jesus was not a stupid man; indeed, as we have seen, he was a spiritual genius. One who saw as clearly as he did must also have known where his destiny led him. His predictions of his coming passion were matters of certainty to him, for he knew the consequences of his dramatic challenge to the accepted and venerated way of life.

All that we have examined thus far shows Jesus' remarkable courage. It is clear in his teachings, stories, healings, and encounters with religious leaders. What will become increasingly evident in this chapter is that the decision made during his agony in the garden was not an isolated act of heroism, but the culmination of a life of constant struggle to be true at all costs to his deeply felt message.

THE TEACHING

We have seen that Jesus' teaching was hard won by inner struggle. We have examined his confrontation with his adversary at the
end of his stay in the desert. This story is so familiar that for many it
has lost its numinous, frightening aspect. It was Jesus' courageous
response to Satan in this situation which established his uniquely effective ministry to those facing evil and inner darkness. After forty
days of intense spiritual work, hungry, disheveled, dirty, tired, and
full of his new dramatic message, he found standing between him and
the world one who would confound him, block his way, and trip him
up. It is quite remarkable that he kept his wits about him.

Things spiritual, be they of God or evil, frighten human beings
because they stretch us beyond our ability to comprehend. The angels
of God who appear to people throughout Scripture usually introduce
themselves with the phrase "Do not be afraid." If a positive spiritual
presence strikes fear in the human heart, the destructive reality Jesus
faced must have been truly fearsome. But Jesus was so God-touched
at the end of his desert stay that he not only was not overwhelmed,
but was able to defeat his adversary in their "discussion."

When Jesus later told the multitudes that they must come to
terms with their opponent in good time (Mt 5:25), he knew of what
he spoke. Not only must outer foes be faced—be they Roman or Samaritan—but first the inner opponent must be known and dealt
with. In fact, as Jesus showed in telling the multitudes to take the
plank out of their own eye before worrying about the splinter in the
other's eye, much of one's battling with outer enemies was camou-
flage, preventing the person from seeing where the true enmity lay
hidden. To see what one hated in the Roman, the Samaritan, the
whore, or the tax collector and embrace it as one's own required great
courage, for the tension caused by facing the inner opponent can be
extreme. To show others their own inner tension as Jesus did required
an even greater act of courage, because people hate being shown a previously avoided truth about themselves.

Another example of Jesus' courage is his teaching in the following passage:

> If you are bringing your offering to the altar and there remember that your brother has something against you, leave your offering there before the altar, go and be reconciled with your brother first, and then come back and present your offering (Mt 5:22–24).

Thus, Jesus taught that to be reconciled with one's brother preceded making an outer offering to God. Imagine how his listeners were shocked by this. Here is one example of several of Jesus' teachings which in some way expanded and sometimes even contradicted what was written in the law. To move beyond literal interpretation of the law and particularly to change it posed a great threat to the people and religious leaders and annoyed not a few of them.

In other teachings Jesus very consciously changed the law. Notice in the Sermon on the Mount that five times he used the formula: *The law says* the following *but I say* this to you. For example, Jesus said:

> You have learned how it was said: you must not commit adultery. But I say this to you: if a man looks at a woman lustfully he has already committed adultery with her in his heart (Mt 5:27–28).

Jesus expanded on the law with these words by making inner condition, not outer act, the determining factor. This was primarily a call to greater responsibility and honesty about sexuality rather than a moralistic statement. Remember that Jesus was speaking to a society which scapegoated people who *misbehaved* sexually. But he knew that even the most law-abiding Pharisee had sexual desires and inner conflicts and that these inner conflicts must be faced.

Or again:

> You have learned how it was said: eye for eye and tooth for tooth. But I say this to you: Offer the wicked man no resistance. On the contrary, if anyone hits you on the right cheek, offer him the other as well (Mt 5:38–39).

Here Jesus went against the deeply embedded Mideastern custom of revenge. He also directly contradicted Scripture which would have enraged many of his listeners and shocked all of them.

Jesus continued:

> You have learned how it was said: you must love your neighbor and hate your enemy. But I say this to you: love your enemies and pray for those who persecute you; in this way you will be sons of your Father in heaven, for he causes the sun to rise on bad men as well as good (Mt 5:43–45).

Remember that his Jewish listeners were an embittered conquered people with a long history of captivity. Not only did Jesus make the impossible and inwardly inconsistent demand to love one's enemy, but he compared that action to God's own actions. Shocking! Astounding! Some in the crowds must have muttered, "He speaks as though he thinks he understands God's ways!" Challenging the law like this could only set him at odds with the religious authorities, and required great courage.

He acknowledged that his teachings cause dissension:

> Do you suppose that I am here to bring peace on earth? No, I tell you, but rather division. For from now on a household of five will be divided: three against two and two against three; the father divided against the son, son against father, mother against daughter, daughter against mother, mother-in-law against daughter-in-law, daughter-in-law against mother-in-law (Lk 12:51–53).

For the Kingdom was happening. In order to help it come into being, he had to risk all:

> Up to the time of John it was the law and the prophets; since then, the Kingdom of God has been preached, and by violence everyone is getting in (Lk 16:16).

Though the law remained, Jesus saw that it was not the final measure. Where keeping all the rituals was seen as the ordered and trustworthy way to God, the way of the Kingdom was overturning all that. Strict adherence to a moral code must give way to radical love.

STORIES

Jesus' parables show his great courage in at least three ways. First, the stories he told were radically different from the other contemporary acccounts of God's ways. He presented a God who could be reached by normal people. The fact that he used everyday examples to portray the Kingdom went against the tradition that the temple was the primary place where God was encountered. This lack of distinguishing between sacred and profane worlds was a major departure from the standard teachings.

Second, his cast of characters were not typical either. In fact, as we have seen, the protagonists and heroes were often downright offensive to his listeners. Importunate widows, crafty stewards, shepherds, wasteful sons, and peasant women were shocking teaching examples. And the healer of healers—the example par excellence of the richest and deepest commands in Jewish Scripture—a Samaritan? This was not only insulting and horrifying to his listeners, it was utter madness—not unlike an American being considered as saving healer of a wounded Moslem in a story told to a group of militant Iranians in present day Teheran. Either Jesus was a naive fool or a brave man willing to risk all to bring about the Kingdom. As we have seen, the dunce cap simply does not fit; one who spoke so clearly in his teaching and stories and who read the signs of the times so well could not have been choosing his examples unconsciously.

Third, he told stories about the powerful religious leaders—in their presence—which could only enrage them. One section of Matthew amply demonstrates this (Mt 21:28—22:14). After his own authority had been questioned (Mt 21:23–27), Jesus related a parable about two sons. The father asked them to go to the vineyard to work. The first son refused and then thought better of it and went; the second agreed to go but then did not. The authorities agreed that it was the first son who did the father's will. Then Jesus said, "I tell you solemnly, tax collectors and prostitutes are making their way into the Kingdom of heaven before you." Like the first son in the story, they appeared to be saying no to God. But having thought about it, having been exposed by Jesus to the Kingdom, they proceeded to try to do God's will. The authorities, of course, were like the second son in their verbal agreement to do God's will. But they had refused to act.

A second parable followed about a vineyard owner who leased his land to tenants who, when he sent the servants to collect his portion of the produce, turned on one after another of them, killing them. Then the owner sent his own son (you might find this a questionable maneuver at that point) and they killed him too. His listeners agreed that the owner would bring those "wretches to a wretched end." Jesus then asked an amazing question: "Have you never read in the Scriptures: it was the stone rejected by the builders that became the keystone. This was the Lord's doing and it is wonderful to see?" The scribes were proud of being considered *experts* of the law. This upstart carpenter dared ask *them* if they had never read this passage from the Psalms!

The final parable of this section in Matthew is about a king who had prepared a wedding feast for his son. The invited guests refused to come and they beat up and killed his servants. The king in his fury dispatched his troops and destroyed the murderers. Then he sent his servants to the crossroads, where all type of unacceptable persons might be found, to invite them one and all to the feast. One man who refused to honor the king and his son by wearing the traditional garment was bound and expelled from the party into the outer darkness.

Jesus seemed to be telling these leaders that they who had been invited and had refused the invitation had given away the Kingdom to the unclean and the misfits and even to pagans. No wonder they were enraged and "went away to work out between them how to trip him in what he said" (Mt 22:15). Wasn't Jesus inviting them in these stories to see the workings of the Kingdom? And wasn't it a courageous act of intimacy to try to show these authorities that they too could get into the Kingdom if only they would change their ways?

HEALING

Four aspects of Jesus' healing ministry demonstrate his courage very clearly. First, his attitude toward disease ran contrary to popular belief. Unlike his contemporaries who were so frightened by illness that they sent the visibly ill from them, Jesus showed no fear of illness. Rather he stood near suffering people and *touched* them, even those who had been untouchables. Somehow he had faith that he would not become victim to the diseases or become unclean. Second, his attitude toward those suffering from illness ran counter to the Deuteronomic thesis that *all* illness was caused by sin. His attitude inevitably angered the authorities. Third, the very act of healing in such a situation required courage. The possibility of failure and ridicule combined with the social censure of the authorities created a tense situation necessitating great faith. Finally, he used healing as an example of the precedence of the Kingdom over all else. By healing on the sabbath and in the synagogue, Jesus brought this challenge directly to the religious authorities in such a way that they could not ignore him.

SCRIBES, PHARISEES, SOCIETY

Jesus showed his courage by confronting the scribes and Pharisees over and over again. As we have seen, the Gospels are full of his criticism of them. He told his listeners not to be like those who make a great show of their "holiness" (e.g., Mt 5:17–20). He attacked their attitude toward ritual uncleanliness. He totally disagreed with their notions of legitimacy and illegitimacy.

Jesus used the scribes and Pharisees as examples in ways that shocked them and his other listeners. In the story of the Pharisee and the publican (Lk 18:9–14) he compared the Pharisee's proud prayer to the humble petition of the despised publican. How astounding it must have been for his listeners to hear that the publican, that greedy Roman puppet, went home from the temple right with God, but that the law-keeping Pharisee did not. Jesus was not one to pull punches, but this challenge and attack on the religious authorities could only make him the center of conflict and endanger him.

BEHAVIOR

Jesus' actions most clearly demonstrate his courage. Not only in acts of healing, but in living out the words of his teachings and stories, the magnitude of his courage was shown. For it is one thing to verbally question the accepted value system and approach to life, but to act out one's challenge puts one at much greater risk. Had Jesus not backed up his words with actions, we would not be so impressed with him.

He taught, for example, that it is wrong to exclude other human beings from fellowship just because they are unclean or of the wrong profession. Had he left it at that and behaved toward tax collectors and sinners as did those he criticized, he would himself have been a hypocrite. His reactions to specific situations revealed that this was just not the case. We will consider two cases in point.

(1) On his way to Jerusalem for the last time Jesus passed

through Jericho. The tax collector Zacchaeus had climbed into a tree so to be able to see Jesus when he passed by. Jesus stopped under the tree, and, as we have seen earlier, he invited himself to Zacchaeus' house. Jesus did here what he expected of others; he broke the social taboo and entered into fellowship with this socially despised person. He did this by his own free choice which, socially speaking, was probably even more inappropriate than accepting an invitation made by a sinner. He was actually *choosing* to be in a conflict situation. Further he declared that Zacchaeus was a son of Abraham, that is, again a member of the community. This was a direct challenge to the scribes and Pharisees who considered the tax collector a pagan (Lk 19:1–10).

(2) In another episode we have already discussed, several scribes and Pharisees brought Jesus a woman who had been caught in "the very act of adultery." As a test, they asked him what should be done with her, for the law required that she be stoned to death. Jesus knew that they were testing him and he started writing on the ground with his finger. Several aspects of this response are noteworthy. Jesus didn't answer quickly. He saw an impassioned group about to destroy the woman and he proceeded slowly. This moment of writing gave him time to consider his response. We have seen how angry he could get with the scribes and Pharisees, but he stopped himself here from responding quickly with anger. Had he called these already enraged men hypocrites, they might have stoned both him and the woman. If you have ever written with your finger in sand, you probably know what a relaxing, centering experience it can be. His writing may have had the same effect on him and permitted his brilliant response to come into his awareness as he prayed quietly for direction. With his words he in effect stood beside the accusers rather than directly attacking them. It is as if he said: "All right then, fellows, the matter at hand here is sin. Well then, if sin is to be punished, let that person who is free of it begin the punishment." Then he bent down and started writing again. What courage it took to do that! There is no fear or anxiety evident. He has in fact turned them back on them-

selves. They must resolve their own position before proceeding, and as Jesus knew, no one who was honest could find himself blameless.

This story has been so often told that the danger of the situation is rarely considered. Jesus did not know if someone would in fact throw the first rock at her; if that happened, she was a dead woman. Looking back down and writing again was a calculated risk. He might have angered them by so easily dismissing their "question." But his courage enabled him to determine what was the appropriate course and then to accomplish it in such a way and with such conviction that they had to deal with *his* challenge first. His calm response in this very tense situation turned their test of him into a test of themselves. This response by Jesus is so typical that people frequently miss his impressive courage in such difficult and frightening encounters.

Obviously, then, Jesus was courageous. Most of his public ministry simply could not have occurred otherwise. John writes that when Jesus was talking to his disciples for the last time before his death and trying to encourage them he said: "Listen: the time will come—in fact it has come already—when you will be scattered, each going his own way and leaving me alone. And yet I am not alone because the Father is with me" (16:32). Thus, we can see that his courage came from knowing that God was with him as he sought to bring God's Kingdom.

10.

The Death of Jesus

The Gospels reveal that Jesus was a wise and good man, a genius with great power, brave, prayerful, and open to his feelings, a magnificent person who was brutally snuffed out in his prime. How are we to look at his passion? What more is there to say than that Jesus followed his truth to the end and gave his life for his friends and for the Kingdom? Regrettably there is much more to say. For Jesus died in a despicable, grotesque and nauseating way. So horrible was death by crucifixion that the Gospel commentators speak only briefly of it. So common a punishment was it that most adults of his time had seen a crucifixion and had no need or desire to have it described to them.

We have so glorified the death of Jesus, so appropriated it as our own victory over sin and death, that we deny its utter horror. We are almost guilty of believing that the end justifies the means. After all, the Christian belief is that *salvation* for all people was gained through this crucifixion—which is certainly a strong case for the end justifying the means. But when what Jesus suffered is examined more closely, it is not so easy to glibly accept this justification. The death of Jesus is celebrated every year during Holy Week and every day in the Eucharist. Literally billions of people have recalled his end. But this constant repetition can have a lulling effect on us, can trick us into not seeing what occurred.

How then shall we examine the death of Jesus that it might

speak to us in a new way? First, we have the four scriptural accounts of the crucifixion. Then there are the historical data dealing with the procedure as followed by the Romans. Also the physiological and archaeological sciences inform us about the actual experience of death by crucifixion. Finally, our own imaginations give us pictures and evoke feelings as we let ourselves participate in the events of his death. Dare we do this? For such examination will be truly upsetting. So horrible a death was crucifixion that not until the end of the fifth century did crucifixes appear as Christian religious symbols, that is, almost two hundred years after crucifixion had been abolished by Constantine. If there is a reason to answer the dare affirmatively, it is this: Jesus handled this gruesome experience in a remarkable and particular way, and there, unfortunately, we can see the power and beauty of the man most clearly.

Let us then begin, hoping for the courage to honestly confront his death. Let us each become quiet and open to the horror which is now before us. Let yourself imagine a complete picture of Golgotha, the hill of crucifixion. Notice the surroundings, smell the air, feel the breeze, hear any sounds coming from this hill of murder.

It may seem like a nightmare on which you embark. It *is* a nightmare that is beginning. Someone dear is about to die horribly and you cannot stop it. The nightmare moves inexorably toward its devastating conclusion.

The four Gospels agree in general on what occurred, though certain discrepancies and inconsistencies appear. Each report includes some of what the others exclude. Together a fairly complete picture emerges and we will draw from all the Gospels as we proceed.

Jesus with his disciples left the place of their Passover feast and his gift of Eucharist to them. They made their way to Gethsemane, to the Mount of Olives, where they slept. Jerusalem was crowded to overflowing with pilgrims during the Passover. All the inns and private houses were full. Likely, near them on the mount other groups and families camped. Without Judas, the authorities could never have found Jesus amid that crowd of campers in the dark.

Jesus left most of the disciples, took Peter, James and John who earlier had gone up the mountain with him, and asked these three to watch with him for a while. A different kind of transfiguration then occurred. His humanity screeched as he realized what he would face. He knew the horrors of crucifixion and his "soul was sorrowful to the point of death." He threw himself on the ground and prayed. Never had his prayer been more fervent or difficult. "Please let this pass me by, Daddy. Please don't ask me to die. But I will do what you want." Three times, Matthew and Mark tell us, he prayed thus. Twice did he wake up Peter, James and John to ask them to be with him. So fearful was he that Luke (the physician) tells us that he began to sweat blood. A rare but documented condition called hematidrosis can occur in cases of extremely violent mental disturbance following profound emotion or great fear. Jesus was terrified. He felt isolated; chills of ghastly fear charged through his body causing the subcutaneous capillaries to swell and then to burst when they came in contact with the sweat glands and blood appeared on his skin.

We do not know much of what happened during his agony. (John does not report it at all.) Of course the eye witnesses fell asleep ("from sorrow," Luke says) but they probably saw some of his struggle and afterward put together what we now have recorded. We have seen that Jesus often prayed by himself. His time in Gethsemane pushed prayerfulness to its limits. Apparently, some contact with God occurred, for he went from great fear (e.g., Mt 25:45) to a sense of strength (Mt 25:46). Something happened within him which *encouraged* him.

Perhaps at the heart of his desperation he heard a response which acknowledged his humanity and evoked his great and passionate love of the Kingdom. Perhaps something like the following was said to him after he *begged* that the cup be taken from him:

Yes, my dear Son, know that whatever you do, I forgive you and love you, even if you do not carry this through, for that is the nature of my love. But carrying it through is truer to the Kingdom. This horrible conclusion makes the fullest statement of the Kingdom so that others can see and be with us. You are with me no matter what. This cup draws others to us.

Such an answer would touch the intimacy Jesus felt for God and for people. So great was his love that this answer could have inspired him to give others what he already had. But such a response showed also the horrible logic of the Kingdom: for deeply loving, for being God-touched and filled, for wanting to share the Kingdom, he must die this horrible death.

It is distressing to consider that God did not "take away the cup." How could this happen? Was there something in the nature of things which prevented God's intervention? Had the lines been drawn such that God *could not* prevent Jesus' death? Or was this ultimate gift that Jesus made fully his own decision? These are excruciating questions about God to which we have no answer. We only know what decision Jesus made.

When the police came to the garden led by Judas, Jesus had already recovered his balance. "Am I a brigand that you seek me so? I was at the temple daily if you wanted me. . . . I am the one you seek. Let the others go. . . . Do what you have to do. It is the reign of darkness."

He was bound and led to the Jewish authorities. (The accounts differ on specific details.) Lies and trumped up charges were brought against him. According to John, he was slapped by a guard who thought he had answered Annas impudently. In Mark and John, he claimed himself as the Messiah. In Luke and Matthew, he let the words be theirs. He was thus charged with blasphemy and condemned to die. It is interesting (though Rome had the power of execution) that the authorities did not immediately take him outside and stone him. Perhaps this was because he had followers whom they did not want to provoke. If the Romans executed him, the authorities could more easily justify their actions. This decision made, he was struck and taunted by his captors and led to Pilate.

The middle of the night is a time when irrational fears most frequently emerge. Other cultures see it as the time of spooks and gob-lins. After his personal ordeal in the garden—where he fully transcended his fight or flight response—he had the long night to consider what was to come. So many times during the night he must have been overcome with fear. His friends were nowhere to be seen except for Peter at whom Jesus looked (according to Luke) as the cock crowed. Not only deserted but also denied—would not his humanity have shuddered within him when he saw how totally alone he was? It seems certain that he prayed fervently and continuously—as he waited, as he was taunted, as he was slugged and pummelled—finding God again and again. God filled his secret place but did not erase his torment. How much more painful must it have been to feel the presence of the loving Abba and be surrounded by hate and disgust! Might he have wondered for moments if he had not totally failed God after all?

The horrible farce continued as he was brought before Pilate. No lover of Jews, a petty Roman official, Pilate apparently saw something in Jesus he admired. Here as before the Sanhedrin earlier, Jesus was silent and would not answer meaningless questions. In John's account (18:36–37), he did proclaim himself to Pilate: "Mine is not a Kingdom of this world." "So you are a king then?" asked Pilate, and Jesus agreed. Pilate claimed he could find no case against him. Possibly his wife's reported dream about Jesus deeply upset him—for dreams were seen as being filled with meaning in those days.

Pilate seemed not to want to crucify Jesus. But the enemies of Jesus, the authorities, stirred up the masses (how easy that is to do!) who cried out demanding that he be crucified. The force with which this unified hatred, this communal fight or flight response, struck Jesus as he watched must have been enormous. Before him, life shouted "No" to the Kingdom in unison. Something larger loomed, emerged from the masses and taunted him. The force of destructive-ness must have seemed like a gaping, growling, laughing monster: "You have lost, Son of Joseph! The Kingdom will stay in heaven.

You and your shouting friends here are mine for eternity! You have failed and now you die!"

Pilate gave the order. Crucifixion waited. The legal preparation for crucifixion was scourging. The person was stripped naked, tied to a column and beaten with a flagrum—a whip with pieces of sheep bone and metal tied to it—to get the festivities started. Already Jesus' skin was tender with surface nerves dancing from his sweat of blood. Already bruises appeared when he was stripped, from his previous handling. It was now the legion's turn—a chance to release some good conquering Roman energy on an inhabitant of stupid superstitious Jerusalem. And so they whipped, and bone and metal met skin with a crash. Waves of pain shot through his body to his brain. His back and legs took on the appearance of ground meat. Each lash grabbed and gouged him—and he began to die.

"What is this? The *King* of the Jews! He needs a crown!" Thorns fashioned into a cap were beaten onto his head and blood poured out onto his face and shoulders. "Give him a purple robe, man! This is a king!"

A spinning, twirling, swirl of pain, rawness, hatred and spittle surrounded him. Blood and sweat burned and blurred his eyes. Somewhere in him continued the prayers, a thin stretching string holding him to love.

"What fun is this? The king says nothing. Ah, send him on, fellows, to his death. Hail to the silent king!" One last kick in the back lifted him to his feet and his royal robes were ripped from the drying scabs which tried to protect his back. His own robe was put on his shoulders. The cross beam, the patibulum, weighing over one hundred pounds was tied to his raw screaming shoulders. Splinters and corners tore into his skin and under guard he was led the short distance to that hill.

That hill—only about one third of a mile away. Too far, too far. He falls once, his face smashed on the rough cobblestones under the weight of the patibulum. Again he falls and still again. "We've got to get help! He's going to die here! We're to crucify him! You, get this cross." It is untied from Jesus' shoulders and given to the Cyrene. Jesus is lifted roughly to his feet and pushed onward.

The hill, Golgotha. The place of skulls. The stipes—vertical pieces of dead wood—stand waiting for the patibuli and their victims. He is stripped; hardened scabs adhere to his robe. A gasp moves through the crowd—and taunts; one must react some way to this. He is offered the gall which numbs but he refuses. The patibulum is put on the ground with Jesus' upper back on it. He grimaces as the dirt, wood, and stones eat into his flesh but he is silent.

His right hand—that once beautiful carpenter's hand—is stretched onto the wood. The nail is ready and quickly driven through his wrist. His thumb strikes his palm wildly, for the median nerve has been hit. Pain screams through his body and shows on his face—but the shout of pain and hatred does not come forth. Then the other hand is fixed and he is lifted onto the stipes and attached there with a nail.

A notice is placed above his head: *King of the Jews*—Pilate's taunt to Caesar's subjects.

The long ordeal begins. The weight of his body pulls on his hands. Soon cramps grab his arms and his whole body. His face turns violet, then deep blue. He is suffocating. Only by lifting himself can he get his breath. But this sends shocks of pain through his arms and his crown is pushed further into his head as he leans back on the patibulum. The other two men are screaming, cursing, raging. The taunts of the passers-by and the authorities sneak into his consciousness between screams of pain. What will he say? What can he say but that he is gasping for a few more breaths in this damned world won over by the forces of destruction?

The Gospels, though reticent, speak differently, report different words. Perhaps Jesus said many other things also on the cross but only these seven phrases are reported.

Matthew and Mark. These two Gospels record but one saying from the cross: "My God, my God, why have you forsaken me?" Is this a cry of despair, anguish and utter defeat? Perhaps. Are the words by the other commentators a cover-up for this total defeat? Again perhaps. But consider: these words are the beginning of Psalm 22. Likely, Jesus continued praying. After what he had experienced it is not surprising that such a prayer would enter his consciousness. So true to his raw experience on the cross is this verse that it burst his silence. So resonant with his soul, so God-emptied did he feel that the fibers of his being screamed out this prayer.

Let me conjecture for just a moment on the nature of God. Jesus claimed to be in Abba-relationship with God. If, as Jesus believed, God was a forgiving parent, might we not imagine that God heard his prayer, immediately responded and granted him death? Of course, no answer can be given. But how would a loving parent respond to her or his child's sense of total isolation? *Kal va homer!*

John. Let us push on, the question of despair unanswered. The Gospel of John focuses on the divinity of Jesus and the control Jesus had over the events of his life. John reports three sayings. First, at the foot of the cross stood Jesus' mother and the disciple he loved— suffering with him his horrible end. Lifting his head, or perhaps in the midst of his smothering, cramped asphyxiation he saw their sorrow and grief and sought to comfort them! "Woman, this is your son. . . . This is your mother." These tender words whisper the strength and power of love. Crushed and destroyed, the sufferings of others amid the jeers evoked this passionate response from Jesus.

Jesus had lost much blood, and this caused what is known as traumatic thirst. He cried out: "I'm thirsty." John, claiming Jesus' control of the situation, said that he did this to fulfill Scripture. In any case, the thirst was a real experience. Notice that this expression also comes from Psalm 22 (verse 15). Perhaps Jesus prayed this Psalm repeatedly, so accurate was it to his own plight.

Finally, given vinegar in response to his statement, Jesus said, "It is accomplished." Bowing his head, his lungs filled with air, asphyxiation occurred, and he gave up his spirit. What was accomplished? All the Scriptures' predictions? Perhaps. Did something happen at that moment? Did destructiveness give its all? Did evil squash him and yet lose? Perhaps a tenuous thread had strengthened. Perhaps having died so horribly, having (miraculously) borne it lovingly, love penetrated where before it had not—to the heart of hatred, to the center of hell—and though it wavered and wobbled, it held. And Jesus, seeing this, could let death be.

Luke. Three more statements are added by Luke. First, after the phony trial, the beatings, the cowardice of Pilate, the desertion by his friends, the taunts and the scourging, the nails tearing his skin and ripping his nerves, what he had before preached he now prayed: "Father, forgive them, for they do not know what they are doing." This first hint from Luke shows that the possibilities of love reach beyond the limits of hatred. If ever one "deserved" to scream and curse and to bring down God's wrath on others, Jesus at this moment did. But something like what he had heard at his agony in the garden must have communicated to him then: "I am with you, Son, in this torture, grieving, groaning, sorrowful—let us turn what is most grotesque, what is shame itself, into a message of forgiveness. Perhaps they will then hear and come with us."

Continually taunted and jeered by everyone, Jesus came up for air and simultaneously heard one thief rebuking the other on his behalf. This thief then asked to be remembered by Jesus in his Kingdom, and Jesus answered "Today you will be with me in paradise." Can a more ridiculous statement in the midst of such torment be imagined? The very strangeness of two crucified men so conversing gives it a ring of truth—though some might suggest delirium if these were the only words spoken by Jesus from the cross. Matthew and Mark both write that "even those who were crucified with him taunted him." Are not these two statements contradictory? Crucifixion was a long ordeal. It is possible that as one of the thieves witnessed Jesus' death, there on his own cross a remarkable transformation happened. Remember that the two crucified thieves suffered their own suffocating horrors. If such a transformation occurred, it is even more remarkable than all the healings and teachings, for there in the midst of hell and death, the Kingdom came into being. Perhaps this thief was the first one touched by Jesus' prayer for forgiveness.

Finally, as he died, Luke tells us that Jesus said the following words: "Father, into your hands I commit my spirit." For this passionate man full of love and intimacy, these words express the return of the prodigal to the one whom he loved above all others. Even torture had not destroyed their relationship.

Those then are the words reported of Jesus the crucified. Perhaps you disagree with the particular understanding presented here. What seems important is that we see the opposites that collided on that hill. Hatred and love met and fought to the death. Hatred won but love conquered. The torture was somehow enveloped by love but should not be forgotten for that. The end of Luke's account suggests, I think, the appropriate attitude to take toward the crucifixion:

> When the centurion saw what had taken place, he gave praise to God and said, "This was a great and good man." And when all the people who had gathered for the spectacle saw what had happened, they went home beating their breasts (Lk 23:47–48).

It is as though Jesus' murder was unavoidable. Either he had to give up his attempts to bring the Kingdom or be destroyed by those who would prevent him. Facing his death as he did was his ultimate gift to the Kingdom. Can we do more as we watch this spectacle than beat our own breasts?

11.

Resurrection

And so Jesus died. How is the person who feels passionately about him supposed to react to this horror? The automatic answer, perhaps, is resurrection. Of course Jesus died in a grotesque way. Of course he suffered terribly. But he was raised from the dead and this is his victory.

But this is terribly unsatisfactory. It too glibly ignores the disgrace of crucifixion. Too quickly it covers the trail of blood. Resurrection cannot be so easily accepted. There is something offensive about resurrection in a way—as though it is a cop-out, a whitewashing of the murder that God allowed.

As I said in the Preface, I feel passionately about Jesus of Nazareth. The more I have come to know about him, the more impressed I am with him. And the less satisfactory automatic resurrection is to me. And yet I need resurrection desperately. I need life to be such that death can be transcended, transformed, accepted. But automatic resurrection is a magic show, a pretense that we understand what is impossible for us to understand.

Just as I feel passionately about Jesus, so too do I feel toward resurrection. Death and hell are realities. There is an abyss that swallows people. Resurrection is an utter necessity. Every mythology that has been recorded has noted this. But that doesn't mean that it is so.

Let me be clear about my position. I long for resurrection to be real. I have experienced moments of resurrection in my own life—through dream, imagination, and relationship. These things I will share later; here I want to provide the framework for discussion. This is not an intellectual exercise but rather an expression "from the bowels." The facts, as I see them, are as follows. Jesus was a remarkable human being, full of power, love, compassion and truth. His was a unique relationship with God that introduced God's Kingdom to humanity. Social, psychological, economic, political and spiritual forces combined to destroy him. Obviously, Jesus saw this destruction coming but he did nothing to avoid it. He died an ignominious death, in disgrace, although apparently even on the cross there were several moments when the presence of the Kingdom was manifest. His death caused observers to acknowledge him as good and to leave Golgotha beating their breasts in agony and deep sorrow. His followers pulled the spikes from his body and, after wrapping him in funeral garments, buried him.

Dead.

Don't move too quickly from that to resurrection. Jesus was dead. The tendency, of course, is to let resurrection charge in like Superman or the Lone Ranger to save the day—and humanity. But that is unfair to the man who has died.

Resurrection is utter paradox. It seems to me that the person who has no doubts about it is a liar, for resurrection is too remarkable an event to be accepted at face value, uncritically.

But how can we approach resurrection critically?

Perhaps we can't. Let me remind you, however, that criticism is not a synonym for objectivity. I doubt that a person can be objective about resurrection. In fact, only by encountering resurrection can we make a judgment about it.

But how?

The Gospels don't tell us much about it—nothing about the event itself. How could they? That was between God and Jesus. About his followers we learn that they were a bunch of doubting Thomases when they heard he lived again. According to Luke, the women who went to the tomb with spices saw "two men in brilliant clothes" who told them Jesus had risen. In turn the women reported this to the Eleven and the others but their story "seemed pure nonsense and they did not believe them" (Lk 24:5–11). At the end of Mark's Gospel, it is written that Jesus first appeared to Mary of Magdala. She then told those who had been his companions and "they did not believe her" (16:11). Next Jesus appeared to two of them in the country. "They went back and told the others who didn't believe them either" (16:12–13). When he finally appeared to the Eleven themselves he "reproached them for their incredulity and obstinacy, because they had refused to believe those who had seen him after he had risen" (16:14). Of course it was hard for them to believe it. They had seen Jesus die. And so with us. Resurrection of the body isn't an everyday event. Admittedly, modern medicine has brought back many people who have had accidents or heart attacks who were for a few moments "clinically dead." But we're talking about thirty-six hours in Jesus' case. And the resurrection occurred without the aid of technology.

How did it happen? I don't know.

What happened? I don't know.

Why are others who follow him not likewise resurrected? Theological discussions notwithstanding, I don't know.

Why is the world, post-victory over evil, still so dreadful? I don't know but evil is still involved.

What is resurrection? I don't know.

Did it happen to Jesus?

This question stops me, gets close to the real issue at hand for me. One part of me cries out, "Yes, yes, yes! I've felt it myself. It is real." I do know that resurrection, almost above all else, matters— because I know that the abyss and despair exist in this life. And so one must find it.

I also know that resurrection presupposes death, that death is an integral part of the resurrection experience. This makes me feel less kindly toward resurrection. I resent the company it keeps.

But so it is. To experience resurrection means that we need to enter the place of death. The tomb where Jesus lies—dead. We need to let resurrection surround us. The Gospels don't give us any data to help us in this. It is rather an individual journey to that place of death at the center of each of us.

Like the Apostles who doubted the resurrection until they had somehow personally experienced it, we are not to be particularly faulted for "our incredulity and obstinacy." My personal experience, in fact, is that until we admit our particular problems of belief about resurrection we can't be touched deeply by the resurrection experience. I, for one, see the "reasonability" of doubting the actuality of resurrection. Simultaneously, however, I am forced to acknowledge certain facts. As I mentioned briefly, the major mythologies of humankind all acknowledge the phenomenon of resurrection. Death/resurrection is one of the deepest and most profound psychological motifs of humanity. The death and resurrection of Persephone, Adonis, Tammuz, Osiris, and Baldur are all mythological examples of this deep human longing. And those who would become healers in traditional societies had to go through a psychological death and resurrection in order to obtain this status. Second, more specifically to our case, after the purported resurrection of Jesus (and the subsequent Pentecost experience) his followers ceased to be a group of cowards who had deserted their master and became instead great heroes for Christ, willing to give their lives to spread the message of the Kingdom. In Chapter 10, I noted that something happened to Jesus during his agony in the garden as he moved from deep sorrow (Mt 25:45) to a sense of self-control and power (Mt 25:46). So too something dramatic happened to the cowardly, resurrection-denying disciples. Something *had* to have happened to have caused such a dramatic change. I hypothesize this to have occurred in two stages. First, their *experience* of the resurrected Jesus brought the disciples into the awareness of the actuality of the power of the Kingdom over death. The myth of every culture of the dying and rising God could truly occur in real life. But that was not enough, for it did not deal directly and intimately with the death at their own center. It was Pentecost that accomplished this. At Pentecost, the Kingdom manifested itself particularly in each individual present—and so successfully that Peter and the others fought for the Kingdom until all of them were killed. Something happened. I don't know what. But that something is what each of us seeks. Once again, the resurrected Jesus showed those who experienced him that God's Kingdom is more powerful than death, that a human being who is *totally* involved in the Kingdom discovers the power of the Kingdom even in death. For his followers, Pentecost personalized the reality of the Kingdom, for there the Kingdom was bestowed on them and transformed them. They became, as it were, the branches of his vine.

The next question is, I think, what about us? Even if we begin to be touched by the power of resurrection and the gift of Pentecost, are we not still on the outside looking in? In my own case as I discussed in the Preface, after first having been overwhelmed by the negative power of destructiveness and then rescued through understanding friendship and the gift of the cross, the Gospels suggested to me the *possibility* of the victory over ultimate destruction. My subsequent studies of Jung, Kelsey, Campbell, Eliade and others helped me to realize that resurrection is a universal human longing. And the fact that my equals, the cowardly disciples, were transformed into heroes *after* their leader was murdered especially encouraged me that resurrection and Pentecost were actual experiences. This, of course, didn't satisfy me because I needed the experience myself. As I reflect upon it now, I see that resurrection is probably, in one sense, a developmental phenomenon. Jesus, from the time of his call to leave Nazareth (and perhaps before) moved toward resurrection. Or, in another sense, many events of his were "minor" resurrections—his stories, healings, times of prayer and his expression of deep emotion were the Kingdom happening, which is resurrection. Still again, resurrection is the realization that one's faith is a correct perception of reality. By this I mean that resurrection is the ultimate "So that's the way it is with life."

And still I am dissatisfied. Too many people have suffered horribly to let God off with an "Ah, well that explains it." Resurrection is, then, perhaps, like the fantasy in Chapter 1 of the inner time of crucifixion when God meets Jesus at the moment of death and Jesus realizes that God is even there in the pit of hell, suffering, waiting with open arms to take Jesus home. For those who have despaired, who have been in hell psychologically, spiritually or emotionally due to outer and/or inner events in their lives, this sense of resurrection rings true. And it is at this level that the despairing, resurrection-starved soul can, as the liturgy has it, "make bold to ask" that God come to that particular place that needs to be redeemed in itself by the straightforward power of resurrection—not by some holy hollow words and promises.

With this in mind let me bring you to an imaginative (and real) encounter with resurrection in my own life. About eight years ago, I dreamed that I was in the tomb at the resurrection of Jesus as it began. Jesus was going to be brought back from the dead—and my reaction was utter terror. It was with this feeling of terror that I awoke. I knew I had to do something with my dream, so as not to lose the meaning of it, so as not to be overwhelmed by my fear of it. So I brought it into prayer, to quiet, to inner reflection, and I met it. The following is an account of that experience.

> Dear Abba, I am upset and "touched" this morning. I feel the need to cast off my concerns and come into the numinous, into my frightening dream of resurrection, in imagination with humility.
>
> I ran from this, forced myself awake (whatever that may mean) and found myself alone in my room and not alone. All negative power seemed gathered around me about to burst upon me at any moment. I prayed but avoided the resurrection which frightened me even more.
>
> Oh, how I fear you! How I fear life which is so much larger than myself!
>
> And yet I want to do your will—given the two choices. The

third choice of avoiding it doesn't seem to be offered. So I will enter the resurrection scene now, praying for your help and Jesus' help, more hoping than believing in the utter transformation beyond my imagination.

It is a dark cave, cold, musty, threatening to such a coward as I. I don't know how I happen to be here, or by what teleportation. But it is cold and I am afraid.

In the darkness I can sense death, and I am horrified that I have retained consciousness, that I should have to know this. Have I died? Do I wait as Lazarus trapped in my death, longing for a release, for an impossible rescue?

Certainly I do. I do. I do.

Please, please find me, bring me life, resurrect me.

My eyes begin to adjust to the dark. Oh why do they become so powerful, so penetrating? I see on the slab dressed in funeral gown my battered, torn, dead Savior. There is no hope of salvation now. There is only complete death and this trapped eternity with my dead Savior. How can I ever survive this death, Abba? Why, why have you forsaken me?

I bend over my dead Savior. Dear brother, Jesus, what have they done to you? You are torn, ripped, sore. And what you have had to bear, I cannot begin to bear for you.

Oh Jesus, forgive the Pharisee in me, the proud saint and righteous man. Forgive the Sadducee in me, who feels victorious now in your death and lack of resurrection. I am not he, I am not the Sadducee. But I cannot deny him.

Oh God, it is unfair that you have promised a Savior and then killed him. I would spit at you for your miserable humor. But I am afraid, Abba, too afraid, too alone to spit, for the spit lands hollow and echoes in this dark prison.

Oh let me die, let my consciousness perish, let all knowledge of this perish with me, for I cannot stand this injustice, this death, this horror. Let all plans for me be forgotten, let me no longer exist. Count me an unfortunate mutation and accept your mistake. For I am not big enough to accept my Savior's death. Now the earth is hollow, now there is only terror, now the creation becomes a horrid joke.

Dear Jesus, dear brother, oh how I love you though I am afraid. How I long for you to live. How I feel that I should die in your place. Oh rise, rise, make the universe make sense. Oh Jesus! Forgive my taunts, my laughter at your magic, my disdain for orthodoxy.

I am here as I am and that is all. I am here where I don't want to be—in the tomb with my Savior. If it is my lack of understanding come to me in my fear, transform me so that I can see you live, undo me, I need you, I want you to live.

Come alive as you are claimed to live. Come into my dead soul. Give it life and make it breathe again. Show it the possibility of glory. And accept my humble, feeble promise that I will be as open as I can, trying not to be possessed by the negative forces which tell me that I am all my life and the center of my universe.

I am willing to give up myself, fearfully in this numinous spot. I feel the power growing. This time I will try not to flee the Hound of Heaven. Come alive through Abba's power. Help me to bear this, for I can bear no resurrection into everlasting darkness. Arise through the power, arise.

It is very quiet. I sit on the floor of the cave staring at him. An eternity of death passes. Suddenly I am confronted with the Power. Suddenly there is an all-encompassing point of light which is everywhere and nowhere. Suddenly Jesus moves and I am utterly, totally, unredeemably afraid.

I want to flee, but, being awake this time, awakening cannot save me. I pray, Abba, your will be done. Make him arise. Save me. Let me die if it is your will but grant me one glimpse of him in his restored life so that I might die peacefully, so that eternity wherever I may spend it will have this experience and knowledge to sustain me.

The cave becomes the Holy of Holies. My fear will kill me, that mystery which saves me is too much for me, will kill me. Please God, let me first see the Life; then do with me what you will.

I feel that I will burst, will become a conflagration of matter, bespattering the resurrection, for I am not up to the Power which restores, which can restore life.

Suddenly there is a pulling upward, an incredible victory over gravity which pulls me out of myself and pulls Jesus off the slab. He is filled with radiance and surrounded by lights which are activities and visions unseeable by my untrained eye.

And then comes a fear that's even worse than before. Will he cast me out, unworthy sinner that I am? Will he send me away?

Jesus, I say, I am here with you. I have witnessed that which I should not. Forgive my trespassing. I could not help it, and seeing you dead drew from me deep prayers for your living.

He stares at me, eyes me knowingly. I would run if there were a place to go. But such a resurrected person could always find me. He stands and comes to me and speaks.

Jesus: Get up, Son. Accept what you have witnessed, the conquering of gravity.

I am so afraid, my legs won't hold me. I try to stand but I cannot. His torn right hand reaches down to me. He grabs my shoulders and lifts me, as easily as he would a baby. And then I am looking in his eyes. There is no judgment there, only love. The love touches me and it is the transformed Power channeled through a human, though no less immense for that. He opens his arms to me.

Jesus: Come, let me hold you.

How unworthy I am. I can never let you hold me.

Jesus: You are so like Peter. So set in your ways but I love you both, you stubborn goats. He would not let me wash his feet. You know my answer. Come.

He puts his arms around me and strokes my head, my hair, my back. I feel all my fears dissolving away. And then I put my arms around him and the dam bursts and I weep into his chest.

Oh I am so glad you live again.

Jesus: And I am glad that you have faced resurrection. It happens once and forever in the hearts of those in pain who seek love. You have found me. I am here, alive in your center, in your very being. I am with you always. There is no need for you to ever die again. You are born again from above. This cave of my death is the cave of your second birth. This is the end of a long process, a getting ready in you for me. I am here. You now begin again the arduous journey but this time not alone. Let us go forth.

Together we push the enormous rock covering the entrance and the beautiful sunshine rushes over us. It is now that glorious point magnified which brings life to the whole world.

And there, a crying woman looks at us and shrieks—there is no gentler word for it—when she sees him. She kneels before him and he pulls her to her feet. Then the three of us go arm in arm in arm down the road to tell the others the good news.

Such power is available, if sometimes difficult to find. It was the life work of Jesus to point out ways of finding this power. Love your neighbor, love your enemy, know that there is a greater enemy, look inside yourself for the problem, love God, pray, have faith, listen to these stories of life, God and the Kingdom—Jesus' whole life was devoted to the Kingdom. In retrospect, we can see (whatever our belief in the actual event may be) a consistency between Jesus' life and the resurrection. Perhaps Jesus was so tuned to God that he didn't need physical resurrection to prove the power of the Kingdom. Perhaps, living already in the Kingdom, the resurrection was a moot point because he was already there. If so, resurrection is pure gift; it is an example of God's magnificent generosity—done in typical Godly fashion. For God, as far as I can tell, is anything but a showoff. First there is the public murder of Jesus. Then a secret resurrection. A murder that is only too easy for us to believe, understand and view. And a hidden resurrection that turned his pathetic team of incredulous, obstinate fishermen, whores and tax collectors into a dominant force in history.

Resurrection, perhaps surprisingly, tells us as much about the humanity of Jesus as anything else that he did. If the resurrection occurred, then it appears that Jesus was right, that Jesus knew the heart of God as he walked the hills of Palestine, that by following the call into the desert and persevering the long spiritual struggle, the Kingdom of God showed itself to him, filled him, changed him into a God person, a so full to the brim with resurrecting love of God person that people who came close to him could drink and taste the Kingdom and begin to live.

I love the man Jesus. Each time I give myself to exploring his life, some truth comes to meet me in a new way—and that is resurrection. Right now, I see something that has never occurred to me in quite the same way before. Jesus was somehow so full of God that he experienced the power that was necessary for resurrection *before* the resurrection occurred. It was this that gave him the courage to live and speak and act as he did. And somehow, because it seems to be the nature of the Kingdom, resurrection is available to us *if* we go to our own inner desert and face ourselves, our demons and God there. Myths around the world and Jewish Scripture had seen this coming for a long time. There is resurrection in life that is dying to express itself. And amazingly, at the heart of life, at the heart of God, where also was the heart of Jesus, we find the longing of our own hearts to live utterly, fully and passionately—even though death, horror, and sorrow still surround and indeed sometimes overwhelm us, because at the heart, finally, are life, God, and our truest selves.

Afterword:
The Paradox of the Narrow Gate

Our stated goal at the outset of this book was to explore the humanity of Jesus so that we might learn more about him, ourselves, and our place in the cosmos. To that end, we have considered those social and spiritual factors that led up to his public ministry; we have examined his unique teachings, his brilliant storytelling, and his powers of healing; we have studied his particular suggestions about how to pray; we have witnessed his expressions of love, anger and courage to the point of death by crucifixion; we have, finally, wondered about and imaginatively entered into his resurrection.

I believe that a coherent picture of the humanity of Jesus has emerged. The motivating force, the connecting thread, the public secret in his life, was his discovery of the awesome welcoming Kingdom of heaven that God offered to him and to everyone. It has grown more obvious as we have proceeded that we cannot begin to understand Jesus' humanity if we do not see the importance for him of bringing the Kingdom to other human beings. Jesus' life in this sense speaks directly to our own lives, for we are the objects of his public endeavors, we are they who are invited to the feast, in whom the Kingdom is striving to come. The humanity of Jesus is thus directly related to our own humanity. This should not surprise us, for his whole public life was given to making this message known to people. We are to go to our secret places of sin, embarrassment, and brokenness just as he did, if we would get into the Kingdom. We are to love those human beings who are to us most despicable—and as we come to love them, so do we come to love ourselves and enter the

Kingdom. We are to leave the wide way, the accepted way, the way that our leaders would have us go, and seek the narrow gate, and if we seek it, we will find it—and we will not go the way of perdition but will enter the Kingdom. We are to take up our crosses, our struggles, our fears, our existential anxieties, our burdens, our hatreds, our longings, our blood, sweat and tears—and follow. And we will carry our crosses through the narrow gate and find ourselves in the Kingdom.

Jesus' message is frightfully frighteningly paradoxical. Leave the pack so that you may find yourself—and others. Find yourself and you will find yourself helping others find themselves. Lose your life and at the edge—just after you have toppled over it—you will find new life. Face that which is most hateful in you and you will discover at your center a love beyond words, images, or your ability to understand or contain it.

Jesus' message is paradoxical, for the Kingdom comes—and all else remains. Disease and death still threaten, anxieties are never fully and finally erased while we walk this earth. The discoveries of the Kingdom emerge in the black hole of Calcutta, in a world threatened by total destruction, in the sewer of a person's soul—and after transformation the sin returns, for we are somehow still unfinished. But Jesus—thankfully—has given the rule of forgiveness: we are not forgiven seven times but seventy-seven and seven million times after that. The arrival in the Kingdom is not the end of a race but the beginning of a powerful mystery.

Jesus' message is paradoxical as we have heard in his prayer—deliver us from Evil, from the Negator, the Destroyer, the Multimegaton Soul-Smasher—deliver us from that which is more powerful than ourselves. And after his victory, after his resurrection, after facing the seething nothingness of destructiveness which somehow exists in God's good world, after he has done it all and shown us the cost, we are invited to follow him. St. Paul says truly that this is folly (1 Cor 1:7)—but this is the call. What mythology has repeated accurately in a thousand different ways, Jesus saw—a dragon guards the treasure, a monster blocks the way, a storm prevents passage, the hordes block the promised land—and we must be true to whatever way is our way, and there, just as Jesus did, we will find the narrow gate. This is the mystery: there is a dragon that we must pass, and even if we are destroyed—even if the Gatekeeper smashes us as we try to pass so that we lie crushed and dying with the goal painfully, agonizingly, in sight and out of reach—even then, as we breathe our last breath wallowing and moaning in our failure, in fact *only* then are we most truly touched by the loving mystery and lifted to new life.

Jesus' message is paradoxical. In one sense, it is simplicity itself. Be yourself, come to know the person that you are, for God loves you, as you are, with your snake-bitten soul. But this is cruel torture, the unfair loveliness of God—to love this? Why, God, not something more lovable, something easier for me to embrace? Then that most paradoxical of answers comes, that impossible answer to the proud, lusty, envious, hateful, lazy creature who is made in God's own image—the answer that Jesus discovered in the desert and in his prayer—"Nothing could be move lovable than you."

Jesus was a particular human being, with a particular background, and with particular experiences of God and other people. Clearly, as we have seen, the deep questions of life troubled Jesus at least as much as anyone else. His search for understanding led him to the threshold of a Kingdom that beckoned him and others—a Kingdom that, unlike other kingdoms, conquered no one and changed nothing, where one's only demand was to accept the invitation as honored guest. This seems to be how Jesus understood our place in the cosmos; we are invited guests. We must find the narrow gate within ourselves which opens us to that place. Jesus was crucified for accepting his own invitation—and survived.

Bibliography

What follows is a list of the books which have been particularly helpful, informative and enlightening to me in the foregoing study.

Chapter 3
Three very complete analyses of Jewish life in the first century have particularly aided my understanding of the social, political and spiritual situation.

J. Jeremias, *Jerusalem in the Time of Jesus*. Philadelphia: Fortress Press, 1969.

A. Edersheim, *The Life and Times of Jesus the Messiah*. Grand Rapids: Eerdmans, 1971.

G. Bornkamm, *Jesus of Nazareth*. New York: Harper and Row, 1960.

Chapter 4
J. Sanford, *The Kingdom Within*. Philadelphia: Lippincott, 1970. Discusses the inner meaning of Jesus' parables from the perspective of Jungian psychology.

N. Perrin, *Rediscovering the Teaching of Jesus*. New York: Harper and Row, 1976. Particularly Part II which discusses the Kingdom of God stories.

J. Jeremias, *The Parables of Jesus*. New York: Scribner's, 1962.

K. Bailey, *The Cross and the Prodigal*. St. Louis: Concordia, 1973.

———*Through Peasant Eyes*. Grand Rapids: Eerdmans, 1980.

———*Poet and Peasant.* Grand Rapids: Eerdmans, 1976.
All discuss the words of Jesus through the perspective of the Mid-eastern peasant. His writing has strongly influenced my interpretation of the longer stories of Jesus. The reader who wishes to delve more deeply into the stories of Jesus is well advised to study Bailey's brilliant books.

Chapter 5
The area of holistic healing and the influence of the mind in healing physical illness is a growing field. The following three books have been particularly helpful to me.

C. Simonton and S. Simonton, *Getting Well Again.* Los Angeles: Tarcher's, 1978.

J. Achterberg and G. F. Lawlis, *Bridges of the Body-Mind.* Champaign: Institute for Personality and Ability Testing, 1980.

D. Bresler. *Free Yourself from Pain.* New York: Simon and Schuster, 1979.

For a discussion of Jesus and healing see M. Kelsey, *Healing and Christianity.* New York: Harper and Row, 1973, particularly Chapters 4 and 5.

For a concise discussion of altered states of consciousness, see C. Tart, *States of Consciousness.* New York: Dutton, 1975.

On the importance of faith in healing, see J. Frank, *Persuasion and Healing.* Baltimore: Johns Hopkins, 1973.

For a simple description of the placebo effect see H. Benson, *The Mind-Body Effect.* New York: Simon and Schuster, 1979.

Chapter 6
For a discussion of the translation of *anaideia* as shamelessness see K. Bailey, *Poet and Peasant,* pp. 125–129.

204 UNDERSTANDING THE HUMAN JESUS

Chapter 8

The rainmaker story is from C. G. Jung, *Mysterium Coniunctionis*. Princeton: Princeton U. Press, 1963, p. 419, note.

The tornado story is from F. Newcomb, *Hosteen Klah: Navaho Medicine Man and Sand Painter*. Norman: U. of Oklahoma, 1964.

Chapter 10

A most powerful account of the crucifixion is found in P. Barbet, *A Doctor Looks at Calvary*. New York: Image Books, 1963.

A provocative, imaginative account of the crucifixion is offered in M. Kelsey, *The Cross*. Ramsey: Paulist Press, 1980.

For suggestions on entering into scriptural study in a group see W. Wink, *Transforming Bible Study*. Nashville, Abington, 1980.